HOW TO GET OUT OF DEBT

OTHER ONE HOUR GUIDES

HOW TO GET OUT OF DEBT

Michael C. Thomsett

IRWIN
Professional Publishing
Burr Ridge, Illinois
New York, New York

Sponsoring editor: Amy Hollands
Project editor: Gladys True
Production manager: Ann Cassady
Compositor: Eastern Graphics
Typeface: 11/13 Century Schoolbook
Printer: Arcata Graphics/Kingsport

Library of Congress Cataloging-in-Publication Data

Thomsett, Michael C.
How to get out of debt / Michael C. Thomsett.
p. cm.
ISBN 1-55623-336-1
1. Debt—United States. 2. Finance, Personal—United States.
I. Title.
HG181.T48 1990
332.024′02—dc20

90–2858
CIP

Printed in the United States of America
7 8 9 0 K 7 6 5 4 3

PREFACE

If you are in debt today, you are certainly not alone. Millions of Americans have problems controlling spending and budgeting from one month to the next. Maybe you need more discipline as a money manager, but the greater problem is a cultural one that we live with every day: We are told time and again in advertisements that success is getting what you want—even if getting it means living far beyond your means.

This book shows you how to take control of your financial present and future. You can gain the peace of mind that comes from conquering even the most formidable debt problems and still afford the lifestyle you want for yourself and your family.

You will discover the techniques of revising spending habits and attitude toward money so that your debt problems will be eliminated and avoided, not just today but in the future as well. Lenders will continue to entice you, because they can stay in business only as long as consumers continue to borrow money from them. You need to escape the destructive cycle that comes from ever-growing levels of personal debt.

This book shows you how to create and operate a family budget that works, get rid of debt, and negotiate with creditors who are threatening legal action. You will also discover methods for:

- Understanding the spending and living habits that led to today's money management problems.
- Creating an immediate emergency plan to identify priorities and urgent problems, as well as action steps to relieve pressure.

- Beginning and maintaining a savings plan to avoid debt in the future, while achieving your personal financial goals.
- Changing your attitudes about money and debt, so that a workable financial plan can be put into action.

This book gives you practical ideas rather than theories. The worksheets, checklists, and techniques offered will help you reduce debt and show you how to plan future spending habits and money management strategies. Best of all, this book shows you to how to think of money in a completely new way, so that you can avoid debt problems in the future. We explain the important difference between "green" money (money you have earned) and "red" money (borrowed funds). We show you why you need to spend income while protecting assets, and why this is the most practical way to overcome debt problems and increase your net worth.

Debt is a destructive force in your life, and when you are not in control, you cannot plan your future. Real success can be measured not by your spending power, but by the amount of control you have over your money. You don't succeed by convincing a lender to increase your line of credit, but by gaining the financial freedom to avoid depending on that lender.

Michael C. Thomsett

CONTENTS

CHAPTER 1

IS YOUR MONEY GREEN . . .
OR RED?

Experience is the name everyone
gives to their mistakes.
—*Oscar Wilde*

Financial freedom. That's what we all dream of achieving. Some of us set the goal of becoming millionaires; others want to earn a salary of $100,000 a year. But real financial freedom doesn't necessarily come just from getting a lot of money. It is the result of controlling your earnings and assets, not having to worry about debt, and being able to enjoy life—not having to put off doing what you want to do.

You might have a clear idea about what you want, but along the way, you've gotten into debt. You've borrowed money to take vacations, buy new cars, or just acquire a mixture of things. You might even be mystified about exactly how you ended up in debt. Looking back over the last few months or years, you probably can't remember exactly where all that money went, and you might not even be able to figure out *why* you needed to spend the money when you did. But there are solutions that you can put into effect to solve these problems and to avoid them in the future.

You are interested in achieving permanent financial freedom, and in escaping the sense of being stuck with debt—that depressing realization that, unless something does change, your situation can only get worse.

You may owe a few hundred dollars and earn a modest income, or, you might owe many thousands of dollars and take

1

home a much larger income. It makes no difference because everything is relative. If you suffer from the lack of financial freedom, you need solutions, and you need to come up with a plan you can put into action now. Otherwise, the problem will never go away. It will be destined to repeat itself, even if you come up with immediate solutions that don't change the spending habit.

We will present a plan that will get you out of debt and keep you there. But first, you should know that you *are* able to control your financial situation. Remember these three truths:

1. You Can Get out of Debt

As long as you are willing to create a workable plan, set rules for yourself, and then follow them consistently, you will eliminate excessive debt from your life. That doesn't mean you will never borrow money; it does mean you will be in charge, and it probably will require changing some habits that only prevent you from reaching your personal financial goals.

2. There Is a Solution

No matter what debt problems you face today, and no matter how much your expenses exceed your income, you will be able to find a solution—even if it takes several years and great effort. In the long run, you will not have to sacrifice quality of life to get out of debt. On the contrary, by taking control, you will improve your life and be happier—not because you will accumulate money, but because you will achieve the financial freedom you seek.

3. You Are Never out of Options

If you believe you're hopelessly beyond help and that you will never escape the borrowing syndrome, think again. People who resign themselves to the belief that there are no choices left become very unhappy because they no longer believe they have choices. They've resigned themselves to what they consider the inevitable. They have given up on the idea of financial freedom. You always have choices, some logical and easy and others extremely complicated, but the choices are there for you. It's just a matter of identifying them, then selecting the best ones for your situation.

YOUR EMERGENCY PLAN

Later on, we'll examine the question, "How did you get yourself where you are today?" By understanding our mistakes, we can avoid repeating them in the future. But for the moment, you're more concerned with what you need to do to solve the immediate problem of being in debt and out of control. Below are 10 steps you can take now to solve the problem and start yourself on the way to financial freedom. These are not just exercises in theory; they're techniques you can put into effect to find answers.

1. Make a List of What You Have

Get three pieces of paper and start listing what you have. On the first page, write down your sources of income: wages, income from your own business, and every other source. On the second sheet, make a list of your assets and their value. If you own your home, write down the estimated market value. List cash, cars, furniture, stamp or coin collections, clothing, jewelry, investments, and everything else you own. Don't forget to list money that other people owe to you. On the third sheet, write down your resources: relatives who might be able to help you financially, the hours you have available to earn additional money, and any special marketable talents you possess.

2. Make a List of What You Owe

Now make another list—all of your debts. Include your home mortgage (or rent you owe), unpaid loans on your car, credit card balances, and all of the other amounts you have borrowed from others.

Compare your two lists. If your assets are worth more than your debts, then you are solvent. It would be possible, although not practical, to sell enough of your assets to pay off all of your debts. But there are two problems with this idea. First, it would probably leave you without shelter and transportation. And second, it wouldn't ensure that you could stay out of debt. The purpose of testing your solvency is to decide whether it will be possible, with the resources at hand, to get yourself out of debt quickly, or whether the task will demand a period of many months or years.

If your debts are greater than your assets, you have a choice. You may come up with a plan to repay all of the debts from future income. Or you can go into bankruptcy and start over again, or at least reorganize your debts so that full or partial repayment will be achieved on a realistic schedule.

3. Get Rid of Unnecessary Expenses

How do you spend your money each month? Can you reduce any of your expenses, or even eliminate some of them? Considering that your immediate plan is to take control of your situation, consider cutting out all unnecessary types of spending including recreational or hobby activities. Remember, this is a temporary measure. If you sacrifice too much for too long, you won't really achieve financial freedom. Putting a stop to spending money on anything but necessities should not be a permanent move, only a change you make until you're more in control.

One form of unnecessary expense you will want to avoid is any additional debt. There are many ways to save someone who's drowning, but giving them a glass of water is not one of them. Don't borrow more money in an attempt to solve the immediate problem; that will only delay you from achieving financial freedom and keep you on the treadmill you need to escape.

Be sure the expenses you eliminate are truly unnecessary. For example, don't stop making payments on your life, health, or auto insurance policies. These are essential because they protect you against losses you wouldn't be able to afford.

4. Come up with a Payment Schedule

List your debts by the amount you owe each month, or by the amount you can afford to repay. Don't worry about how long it will take to erase these debts completely. Concentrate on creating a plan you can manage. Start with the immediate necessities—food, housing, utilities, and transportation. Secondary necessities like clothing, car and home maintenance, and insurance should be allowed for with a monthly allowance you will set aside. Detailed budgeting ideas and techniques are explained later in the book.

5. Increase Your Income

At times, the most obvious solutions don't occur to us because we're too close to the problem. For example, have you thought about taking a part-time job to bring in more income? Your spouse can work another job as well. This is another temporary measure. All of the take-home pay you earn from a second job should go into one of two places: repayment of debt and savings (see step 6 below).

Depending on the amount of debt you owe, it's important to put a time limit on this temporary measure. Otherwise, you'll spend all your time working, which is replacing one problem with another. Financial freedom is tied directly to the way you use your time and the flexibility you have in being able to control time. If you are always at work, you have no time to yourself and no financial freedom at all. So a second job should be an immediate change that you will want to cancel as soon as possible in the future.

6. Start a Savings Plan

You might ask, "What does opening up a savings account have to do with getting out of debt?" In fact, it's one of the most important ways to change your spending habits and start on the road to financial freedom. The sooner you start putting a few dollars every month into a savings account, the sooner you will be able to take control of your financial life. Putting money regularly into a savings plan is a discipline that goes hand in hand with control over debt. We'll talk about the importance of methodical savings in greater detail later in the book.

7. Get Professional Help

If you need counseling to help identify your assets and debts, make an appointment with your banker or a financial counselor, but be careful when you make your selection. You certainly don't want to pay a huge fee for a few words of advice. What you need now in some practical, specific help in defining the scope of the problem you face, and identification of the most realistic solutions and alternatives available to you. You might get free advice from your local banker, credit union officer, or financial planner (some planners offer free initial consultation). You can also seek free advice from financial professionals who are friends of the family, or even family members.

8. Contact Your Creditors

This step is the one most often overlooked; but it is essential to taking control. In most instances of default or late payment, the creditor's problem is getting people to cooperate, even to communicate. Creditors are accustomed to evasive action—people not answering letters and phone calls, promising to pay soon, or saying, "The check is in the mail."

What should you tell your creditors? Be direct and honest. Tell them three things:

   a. I am having a problem, but I'm taking immediate steps to solve it.
   b. I am going to repay the entire debt.
   c. I want to cooperate with you to come up with a realistic repayment plan.

Then present your proposed plan. Even if you will only repay a few dollars each month, that's better than nothing at all. Most creditors will be happy to work with you, as long as you make the contact and offer a commitment in good faith.

9. Keep the Promises You Make

Your emergency plan involves making promises that must be kept. The first set of promises are those you make to yourself—establishing a number of steps you will take to get out of debt. The second set of promises are made to your creditors. In both cases, your plan will work *only* if these promises are kept. So your plan should be realistic and practical, and you must be prepared to follow through.

10. Put Your Plan into Action—Today

Don't delay putting your plan into effect. As long as it will work and as long as you will be able to keep your promises, the sooner you act, the better.

Your 10-step emergency action plan is summarized in Figure 1–1.

IDENTIFYING THE PROBLEM

Once your emergency plan is put into effect, your next step is actually to change your spending habits. That's no easy task. We all suffer from the debt syndrome, which is reinforced in the messages we receive from advertisers—get what you want now, want and get even more, don't wait or you'll miss acquiring what you *must* have, borrow as much as you want, a penny borrowed is a penny earned.

The debt syndrome arises because there is a conflict between two types of freedom. The financial type, with which you will be able to acquire things you really do need and want, can be achieved if you're able to create your own simple but precise financial plan. The other type is the freedom to get something now, even if you can't really afford it. This isn't really freedom, but a trap, and one that you can fall into easily.

Example: The couch in your living room is ragged and old, and it's time to get a new one. You visit a local furniture store and find a couch you like for $500. The salesman mentions that

FIGURE 1–1
Emergency Action Plan

---

1. Make a list of what you have.

2. Make a list of what you owe.

3. Get rid of unnecessary expenses.

4. Come up with a payment schedule.

5. Increase your income.

6. Start a savings plan.

7. Get professional help.

8. Contact your creditors.

9. Keep the promises you make.

10. Put your plan into action – today.

you can buy whatever you need today, and there will be no payments and no interest charged for six months, so you buy an entire living room set costing about $2,500.

In this case, you started out with a very specific idea and ended up spending five times as much for things you didn't really need. Why? Because it was easy and convenient. The real trap is that, when payments are deferred (or, when they're very low each month), the illusion is that it's not costing as much.

The mistake is in thinking not of the cost, but of the convenience. It's easy to find yourself believing that borrowing money or deferring repayment is the same thing as not paying for something.

Example: A major chain store places tags on appliances showing the monthly payment in large letters, and the total price in very small letters. In comparing one refrigerator to another, you find yourself looking not at the cost, but at the relative affordability of monthly payments. You forget all about the total cost, which will include interest each month. Chances are you didn't even check with the competitors to see if a better deal was available somewhere else.

Some very successful stores earn their profit not from selling goods alone, but from the combination of pricing and financing. A careful price comparison will show that some goods are marked well above competing prices, but the financing terms are so easy, and getting credit is so immediate and convenient, that the higher price is not a problem. In fact, price is often forgotten altogether. A good number of shoppers are looking for a monthly payment bargain rather than a good price.

These are only a few of the problems you face as a consumer in a society that tolerates and even encourages debt. If you want things now, and if you don't want the inconvenience of having to pay cash, the whole arrangement can be handled very easily—just sign on the dotted line and we'll send you a payments book.

After doing that a few times, you could end up with a lot of payment books, and with several monthly statements from credit card companies and department stores. As debt repayment takes on an ever-growing percentage of your available income, the trouble begins.

SETTING UP YOUR DEBT POLICY

A financial plan begins when you make rules for yourself. Consider including these suggestions as some of your personal financial rules and guidelines.

1. Borrow Money Only As a Last Resort

Make it difficult for yourself to go into debt. Constantly question convenience and easy terms and plan your expenses carefully. If you commit yourself too casually and without thinking about your future budget, it's fairly easy to get in over your head. Before accepting the assumption that buying on credit is "the way it's done," look for other ways. Some purchases must be made on credit, such as a first home. In that situation, debt might be unavoidable. But a good many purchases can be delayed or paid for in cash, or might not have to be made at all.

2. Know When You're Going into Debt

Many of our modern forms of debt are packaged to look like something else. "Convenient, affordable terms" is a soft way of saying, "Pay more but over a longer period of time." And for homeowners, equity lines of credit that make it easy to get money should be recognized as a form of borrowing. Don't be swayed by lenders' ads scolding you for "leaving your equity idle" or advising you to "put your equity to work." Using your own equity requires that you go into debt, and that means the loan has to be repaid.

3. Never Buy Impulsively

You might not plan to go into debt, but end up there just the same. Some of the most expensive purchases are made this way. You might enjoy occasionally setting aside a sum of money just to spend—even on things you don't really need. That's a form of reward that you deserve to give yourself. But when you go out for a Saturday drive and end up buying a $900 television you don't really need, or a $13,000 car you didn't know you wanted, then you're buying on impulse.

4. Develop Smart Spending Habits

Organize yourself so that you spend money only according to your plan. For example, shop for most of your groceries once each week, using a precise list. Never do your shopping when you're hungry; go to the store after dinner instead of before.

Plan major purchases far ahead of the time you begin looking. For example, if you decide the time is coming to buy a new car, don't start visiting showrooms and car lots to "get an idea" of price. If you do, you might just end up signing the papers now, when your plan called for waiting a few more months. Remember, the salesman's job is to get you to buy today. And it's easy to overlook or forget the importance of timing.

5. Pay Back What You Owe Now

Don't take on more debt until you have repaid what you already owe. You have probably seen other people make this mistake. They are deeply in debt already, but go further into debt, aggravating the problem. Before you take on more monthly payments, pay back what you already owe.

6. Don't Borrow to Consolidate Other Debts

Some people respond to ads for "easy money" with the idea of consolidating—borrowing money and using it to pay off a number of current debts. For example, you are making payments of more than $400 per month on department store and credit card accounts. The total owed is $3,000. You could borrow $3,000 and pay off all of those debts, reducing your monthly payment to less than $100 per month for the next three years.

This might seem like a smart idea, until you think about what is likely to happen. Within six months, your department store and credit card balances might be back up to where they are today—then you'll owe twice as much money. By consolidating, you will have increased your debt rather than reducing it. The only time consolidation works is when you are certain that the old debt won't be repeated—and that usually means closing out your accounts and not reopening them or replacing them with others.

These six suggested rules are summarized in Figure 1–2.

BORROWING WISELY

There are times when debt is not only acceptable, but a smart idea. Properly controlled, going into debt can help you achieve financial freedom, but only if you're working from a precise plan and budget.

Example: Real estate values have been rising steadily over

FIGURE 1–2
Staying Out of Debt

1. Borrow money only as a last resort.

2. Know when you're going into debt.

3. Never buy impulsively.

4. Develop smart spending habits.

5. Pay back what you owe now.

6. Don't borrow to consolidate other debts.

the past few years in your area. You have enough money saved up for a 20 percent down payment. If the real estate price trend continues, a home you buy today will increase in value over the years. As long as you can afford to make mortgage payments every month, you will gain personal security as well as financial freedom because you will be building home equity over time.

There is an absolute distinction between borrowing wisely and losing control over your personal finances. Remember that there are two types of money in our society: green and red. Green money is represented by cash you earn as an employee or owner of your own business, or from return on investments you make. It is also home equity, the balance of savings, retirement funds, and the assets you own above and beyond what you owe. Red money is the credit you accumulate—your debts.

An interesting comparison can be drawn between green

and red money, and this comparison points the way to wise borrowing. Green money can be spent or saved, controlled, and used to take care of your recurring obligations (food, rent, transportation, clothing, utilities, recreational activities). Red money, though, is more likely to evaporate like so much steam. Red money can be used wisely so that you increase the value of assets rather than use them up.

Example: You have an outstanding mortgage loan on a home that is increasing in market value, above the equity you're gradually accumulating. In this case, red money (debt) is being used to help increase the value of your assets.

Example: You borrow money to consolidate bills. But a few months later, the bills have returned and you still owe money to your lender. In this case, borrowed money has only made your situation worse.

The guideline for borrowing wisely is an easy one to remember:

> *Whenever you borrow money, it should*
> *be used to increase the value of assets.*

If you borrow with that standard in mind, you will never again have a problem with controlling debt. Borrowing can increase the value of assets in the following ways:

Example: A homeowner commits to a second mortgage of $30,000, and uses the money to add a fourth bedroom and a second bath. By the time the home is sold, the improvements have added $40,000 in market value.

Example: Your car is six years old and you have had a number of mechanical problems. Average repair bills are running about $200 per month, and seem to be on the increase. You trade in the car on a new one, and must now make payments of $125 per month for the next four years. Since you've been paying $200 per month in repair bills, you decide to keep your budget at the same level. Subtracting payments of $125 from the $200, you begin placing the extra $75 per month in a savings account. In this way, you're still paying out $200 per month, but part of it is still yours.

Example: You have run up balances on several credit cards over the past year. Monthly payments are about $300. You borrow enough to pay off all of the outstanding balances, and must now make monthly payments of about $100. You take two additional steps: First, you cancel and destroy all of your credit cards, resolving to use cash for all future purchases. Second, you begin saving $200 per month (the difference between the level of payments you've been making, and the payment on the new debt balance).

SEPARATING ASSETS FROM INCOME

In many of our examples, we have proposed putting money into savings. This idea will keep you out of debt and help you achieve financial freedom in several ways:

1. It starts you thinking about saving money instead of spending it—an essential change along the road to financial freedom, and the beginning of a new habit that's much healthier than depending on borrowed money.

2. It creates a reserve for future emergencies. If and when those emergencies do arise, you will have the funds (in green money), and will be able to avoid further unexpected debt.

3. It builds an element into your budget for the methodical accumulation of assets, which otherwise cannot be achieved.

Taking control of your financial life requires making a distinction between two forms of wealth. First is the kind you spend every month—income you earn that goes right into housing, food, clothing, and other necessities. Second are the assets you accumulate and control, like a home, furniture and clothing, investments, retirement funds, and a savings account.

The distinction can best be defined by remembering this important rule:

Spend income but preserve assets.

If you have had a chronic problem with debt, chances are you haven't been able to accumulate or preserve assets.

Example: You have borrowed your home equity through a convenient equity line of credit and used it to pay for a new car of television, or an expensive vacation. That's a form of spending your assets. It doesn't matter what your home is worth if you've drawn out your equity and spent it.

Example: You have sold off an investment to pay bills, only to have similar bills again within a few months. You have wiped out your green money, only to replace it with red money.

When you recognize that assets are permanent and should not be used for immediate bills or other purchases, you have taken the first step toward financial freedom. Ultimately, it's not what you earn that counts—it's the value of the assets you control that decides how free you are or could be.

We have emphasized savings because that's the way to start building an asset base. If you don't work from a monthly budget, it's unlikely that you'll have anything left over for savings. So you need to develop a savings plan and follow these steps:

- Think of savings as a necessity, and put money into your account *before* deciding how much to spend on other things. In other words, pay yourself first, then pay everyone else.
- Add to savings when your budget changes. For example, you have been paying $50 per month on a loan. It's finally paid off, but instead of spending the $50 per month on other things, continue making the payment each month. Instead of sending it to a creditor, pay yourself. And when you receive a raise at work, put at least some of the extra money into savings, rather than allowing your budget to grow with your income.
- Avoid using your savings for month-to-month expenses. It should be used only for emergencies and to avoid going into debt. But the real purpose of the savings account is to build up your net worth (the difference between what you own and what you owe). That's achieved by leaving the savings on deposit or by investing it wisely.

Your financial freedom begins when you develop a personal financial plan. You can develop this plan and put it into effect on your own, and without needing any special financial knowledge you don't already possess. The plan is nothing more than your personal goals and standards placed on a timetable and based on your income and available assets.

At first, your plan will be built around the idea of getting yourself out of debt. That's the most immediate concern. But in

CHAPTER 2

ANY ROAD WILL GET YOU THERE

> When the foundation of a pyramid
> erodes, the top can still be
> supported on nothing but money.
> —*Laurence J. Peter*

The title of this chapter is the second half of an old saying: "If you don't know where you're going, any road will get you there." That's what goal setting and financial planning are all about—taking charge of your financial affairs, looking ahead, and deciding what you need to do right now to reach your goals.

You start by defining what you want and then breaking down your goal into specific steps. Essentially, that's all financial planning is, nothing more than a schedule of steps, timing of actions, and setting of rules for yourself and for your family.

Financial planning is often thought of as a sophisticated and somewhat mysterious process aimed at helping people accumulate wealth, plan for a comfortable retirement, offset the effects of inflation and taxes, and build an investment portfolio. But you're in debt today, so your immediate plan should be to get rid of those debts and stay out of debt in the future. That's the most important goal right now. You may want to buy a home (or a bigger home), plan for your children's college education, start your own business, or plan your retirement. Those are longer-term goals, and we will discuss them later. Eventually, you will be ready to work on a plan that looks far ahead. For now, though, let's come up with a plan that will get rid of the problems that are immediate and critical.

THE THEORY OF GOAL SETTING

You've probably heard others say, "Sticking to a plan takes a lot of discipline." In fact, you might have said that yourself. But in fact, it's not really a matter of exceptional discipline that will help you get out of debt. The real secret is in developing a simple plan and schedule, including clear, precise goals that you want to reach, and then following the course you've set for yourself. Instead of demanding superhuman discipline, the process really removes all of the indecision from the process of handling money. It simplifies matters and increases your freedom when you have a specific plan, rather than restricting you or limiting what you can do.

Instead of having to decide which bills to pay and which ones to put off, your plan is set up to manage and coordinate payments. For a lot of families, the two worst days of the month are the 15th and the 30th. On those days, paychecks arrive and are put in the bank. The bills are stacked up, and the decision has to be made. Then the trouble begins. Spouses disagree and begin to argue. Both feel trapped because the bills add up to more than the money. Beyond the question of what should be paid or delayed, there's obviously nothing left over for recreation. People feel trapped when they're controlled by debt, rather than the other way around. It might come out as anger and frustration at each other; but the real problem is *lack of control.*

Solving this problem requires a budget, to be sure. And we'll get into that in the next chapter. But first, you need to decide what's important to you during the coming year—what do you want to accomplish, given the limits of your income? Is your goal realistic? And what steps can you take right now to begin achieving the end result? How big is the problem, and what has to be done right now to solve it?

That's how you set a goal—by first defining the problem. There's nothing mysterious about it, but you will gain a great amount of power and control by solving problems through goal setting. Successful people know the secret: when they set goals and track them faithfully, they get results. Once you put your goals down on paper and pick a date to achieve them, something very interesting and rewarding starts to happen. You reduce your problems, you escape the sense of hopelessness, you relieve that twice-monthly pressure, and you begin to see a solution as it develops.

There is no magic fix involved. In fact, debt is a perfect topic for goal setting. With a schedule for eliminating debt, you achieve a degree of progress every time you make a payment. But in order to really achieve a constructive result, you need to follow these rules:

1. Once a goal is set, don't abandon it.
2. Resolve to avoid any new debts, or you will defeat your purpose.
3. Review your goals every three to four months and revise them. Your financial status and personal priorities will change over time, and you need to alter your immediate financial plan as those changes occur.
4. Base every financial decision on your goals and always operate based on the plan.
5. Don't relax when you get near the end. See it all the way through. Avoid the temptation to let a few bills go longer than you first intended.
6. Be ready to set new goals. As you near the achievement of today's goals, start reviewing over again.

SCHEDULING REPAYMENTS

We'll get back to your goals later. But first, you need to understand the scope of the problem. Then you'll be able to come up with a schedule to wipe out your debts. It doesn't matter how much you owe. Whether it's a few hundred dollars or several thousand, what you need to do now is to list your debts and come up with a preliminary repayment plan.

You will revise the repayment schedule later, when you have put in more work in describing your goals, and when you've completed your family budget. The process you'll go through takes place in several steps:

1. Come up with a preliminary repayment schedule that defines the problem and gives you a starting point for setting your high-priority goals.

2. Define your short-term goals by deciding what you want to accomplish in about one year. It's not enough to say that your goal is to "get out of debt." That's an overwhelming problem. What you need is a precise schedule you can follow month to month, a breakdown of the bigger problem into manageable, bite-sized chunks.

3. Prepare a budget. The best way to devise a realistic budget is described in the next chapter. You need to coordinate and control repayments, spending habits, and debt, all within the budget. The entire matter is limited by income, of course; the purpose of the budget is to gain and keep control.

4. Revise the repayment schedule to fit your budget. Remember, the first repayment schedule you make up is preliminary—it's purpose is to define the problem. Once your budget is completed, you will need to modify the schedule.

Once these steps have been completed, you will have your immediate, short-term plan in place. Then instead of having to brace for the big decisions on the 15th and 30th of each month, there will be nothing to argue about, no tough decisions to make, and no struggle for control. The schedule and the budget have already determined how much will be paid to each creditor.

Now to the first step: listing and scheduling your bills. Figure 2–1 is a worksheet for this. You might need a longer sheet to list your debts, but don't let that distract you. The longer the list, the more valuable it will be to go through this exercise.

Don't try to crowd all of your repayments into six months or even into the first year. If your debts are high, you will need to take more than one year to reach your goal. That's not a problem. Remember, the important thing is to get the ball rolling, to begin making constructive progress, to solve the problem. List the minimum amount you can pay each month, remembering that you will not acquire any additional debt from this point forward.

Example: You prepare a list of the following debts:

	Total Owed	Minimum Payment
Credit card #1	$4,496	$134
Credit card #2	665	16
Store card #1	1,196	34
Store card #2	130	20
Auto loan	2,520	120
Bank loan	783	87
Total	$9,790	$411

A preliminary schedule might consist of simply listing the minimum payment each month for as long as it will take to eliminate all of the debt. But perhaps you already know that your income won't take the burden of paying $411 every month. The maximun you can pay is $325. You will need to reduce monthly payments by $86 just to break even each month. You decide to cut all of the minimum payments in half except the auto loan and bank loan. When you have adjusted your schedule based on your budget, you should also contact those creditors to whom you will pay less than the minimum, and tell them your plan. Keeping in touch with your creditors is essential if your financial plan is to work. The tentative schedule now is:

	Total Owed	Minimum Payment	Monthly Payment
Credit card #1	$4,496	$134	$ 67
Credit card #2	665	16	8
Store card #1	1,196	34	17
Store card #2	130	20	10
Auto loan	2,520	120	120
Bank loan	783	87	87
Total	$9,790	$411	$309

The schedule can now be prepared:

FIGURE 2–1
Repayment Schedule

Repayment Schedule

DEBT	MONTH					
Total						

DEBT	MONTH					
Total						

Repayment Schedule

Debt	Jan.	Feb.	Mar.	Apr.	May	Jun.
Credit card #1	$ 67	$ 67	$ 67	$ 67	$ 67	$ 67
Credit card #2	8	8	8	8	8	8
Store card #1	17	17	17	17	17	17
Store card #2	10	10	10	10	10	10
Auto loan	120	120	120	120	120	120
Bank loan	87	87	87	87	87	87
Total	$309	$309	$309	$309	$309	$309

After nine months, the bank loan with payments of $87 per month will be paid off. That amount can then be spent in accelerating repayments on the other debts. After nine months the debt picture will look like this (not allowing for interest creditors will add to outstanding monthly balances):

	Total Owed	Minimum Payment
Credit card #1	$3,893	$134
Credit card #2	593	16
Store card #1	1,043	34
Store card #2	40	20
Auto loan	1,440	120
Total	$7,009	$324

A revised repayment schedule could be:

Repayment Schedule

Debt	Oct.	Nov.	Dec.	Jan.	Feb.	Mar.
Credit card #1	$134	$134	$134	$134	$134	$134
Credit card #2	16	16	16	16	16	16
Store card #1	34	34	34	34	34	34
Store card #2	20	20	0	0	0	0
Auto loan	120	120	120	120	120	120
Total	$324	$324	$304	$304	$304	$304

With your nine-month revision in mind, when you contact creditors and propose paying less than the minimum, you should also give a finite time limit. For example, you write to credit card #1, and state: "The monthly minimum is $134. I will pay one-half that amount, or $67 per month, for the next nine months. I will then raise my monthly payment to $134."

There is no guarantee that all of your creditors will agree to your proposed changes. In some cases, you might have to adjust your schedule and make the required minimum payment, just to avoid dealing with a collection agency and other pressure. However, most creditors will respond favorably when someone explains their problem and promises an ultimate solution. If their choice is never to be paid at all, they will be willing to work with you until the problem is resolved.

When your repayment schedule has been fine-tuned and adjusted with your budget in mind, you're on the way to solving your debt problems. The amount you need to set aside each month for reducing debt is the total in each month's column. Those payments will be made faithfully. That's an important rule to set for yourself. Once you establish a plan and communicate it to your creditors, you must be ready to keep your promise.

HOW GOAL SETTING WORKS

Remembering that the repayment schedule will be fine-tuned later on, we now have a starting point. When your debts existed as an ever-growing pile of warning notices and unopened envelopes, they were just a problem. Now, listed on a schedule, they're a *defined* problem. And that's a big difference.

The problem is defined not only in its scope, since you probably knew already about how much debt was there. It's also defined in terms of a solution. For example, if you have scheduled your debts for repayment in 15 months, that's your target date. Assuming your budget can handle the level of monthly repayments, you will reach your goal in 15 months. (If you adjust the schedule later and end up needing 24 months, you still have a tangible, specific target date.)

You have a goal. That's what counts at this point, and that's what will make the difference. You won't have to remain in perpetual debt, and, by following your plan, you will escape the debt syndrome once and for all. Goal setting is the first step in taking control over your finances.

Once the schedule is coordinated with your budget, you will eliminate the apprehension of confronting that big pile of envelopes twice each month. You will still have to face problems, like the unexpected bill that pops up now and then—repairing the car, replacing the jacket your child lost at school, or paying the plumber. Those problems will be worked out in your budget, as you'll see later. The important point here is that, with the repayment schedule, you are now in control. You have a clear direction and purpose, and you will reach your goal.

Goal setting does make all the difference. It gives you the path to take that will get you to a specific result. Now that you know where you're going, you also have the road in sight. You will have the comfort and satisfaction of seeing a small degree of progress each month in gradually following the road to your goal, and in reaching that goal and getting completely and permanently out of debt.

That's how goal setting works. It not only eliminates the problem, it also gives you a sense of accomplishment at each step along the way. When you're in debt and feeling hopelessly out of control, it seems there's no solution. The bills just get higher, and income never seems to catch up. In that situation, you can't help but feel out of control and trapped. The real problem, though, is the same problem that led to debt problems in the first place—*not* having a goal.

SHORT TERM AND LONG TERM

If your goals are to work, they have to be realistic, so you have to operate under two limitations. First, your repayment schedule has to work based on your budget and income. Second, you need to emphasize the immediate problem and, for now at least, delay what you'd like to achieve much later on.

Divide your goals into two sections, immediate or short

term, and long term. The short term can mean one year, two years, three years, or whatever it will take to get yourself out of debt. Other short-term goals might include finding a different job, convincing your boss to give you a raise, or creating a working family budget. The idea of dong away with immediate problems is only the most obvious short-term goal. Long-term goals can include buying a home, paying off the mortgage debt, starting a retirement account, or funding college educations for your children.

A goal only works if you give it a deadline. Start by listing your personal short-term goals, and picking the date you expect to achieve them. Use a list like the one shown in Figure 2–2.

Some of the things you want to achieve can't be given deadlines. For example, you might say, "I will not take on any new debts" or "I will stop spending money carelessly." These are not goals, but sensible rules you set for yourself. They can't be included as goals or even treated in the same way, because there's no deadline. Of course, they should be incorporated in the plan if the plan is to work. Perhaps the goal to eliminate debts can be expressed with these rules in mind:

> "I will pay off my existing debts, and, at the
> same time, I will not take on any new debts
> or spend money outside of my budget."

Then you assign a deadline based on your repayment schedule. In this way, the goal (to pay off existing debts) is scheduled and has a final deadline. And it's expressed in the context of your own rules.

Your long-term goals have to be put on the back burner until your debt crisis has been brought under control. That doesn't mean you ignore or forget what you want in the future, only that you can't deal with these matters until the crisis has been brought under control. Still, you should make a list of those goals and begin planning to achieve them.

Use a list similar to the short-term list, but estimate the deadline. This deadline has to be very tentative for now, because by the time you begin earnestly concentrating on long-term goals, everything will be different. You won't have a debt problem, you might be earning more money, you certainly will be saving more, and your goals might even change.

FIGURE 2–2
Short-Term Goals

Short–Term Goals

1. _____
   _____
   _____
   Deadline _____

2. _____
   _____
   _____
   Deadline _____

3. _____
   _____
   _____
   Deadline _____

4. _____
   _____
   _____
   Deadline _____

5. _____
   _____
   _____
   Deadline _____

Figure 2–3 is a sample of the list for long-term goals.

THE GOAL TEST

If you are single, defining goals is entirely up to you. There should be no conflict about what needs to be done, what is the highest priority, or how long it will take to reach your goal. But if you're married, agreeing on the definition of the problem and solutions might not be quite as simple.

There is no point in starting an emergency financial plan until you and your spouse have agreed on these points:

- The most important goals.
- The scope of the problem.
- The time required to solve the problem.

FIGURE 2–3
Long-Term Goals

Long-Term Goals

1. _____

_____

Estimated deadline _____

2. _____

_____

Estimated deadline _____

3. _____

_____

Estimated deadline _____

If you try to solve your problems without first agreeing on these points, you won't succeed. In trying to arrive at a definition, one spouse will have to submit to the goals and standards of the other, or you will need to compromise at a point that both of you can accept.

You will run into problems if you don't go through this compromise discussion before putting your plan into action; in fact, the dialogue should be thought of as part of the planning process. For example, you might set up a repayment schedule and budget, including the rule that you will spend only within the budget and won't take on any new debt. But if your spouse is out charging power tools, clothing, or other luxuries, that defeats the entire plan.

You and your spouse can define your common problems and goals by taking the goal test. On separate pieces of paper, each of you should answer these questions:

1. What is our most important short-term goal?
2. What is our most important long-term goal?
3. How much money do we owe today?
4. How long will it take to get out of debt?
5. What is our net worth?
6. Who should control the money in this family?
7. How much can we afford each month for: debt repayments? housing? food? savings?

Compare your answers, using the worksheet in Figure 2–4.

Most couples will find that there is a wide gap in many, if not all of the answers. Before your plan can work, you will need to agree to the answers or compromise so that both of you can accept the rules by which your plan will be operated.

Understanding the most important short-term and long-term goals is a basic requirement. You can only work toward the goal when you agree on the goal. There's a good chance that neither spouse knows exactly how much debt you have; and until you both do, the problem can't be defined or solved. It's also necessary to agree on how long it will take to get out of debt; otherwise, any schedule will be unsatisfactory to one or both of you.

FIGURE 2-4 Goal Worksheet

Goal Worksheet

DESCRIPTION	RESPONSES		COMPROMISE
	ONE	TWO	
What is our most important short-term goal?			
What is our most important long-term goal?			
How much money do we owe today?			
How long will it take to get out of debt?			
What is our net worth?			
Who should control the money in this family?			
How much can we afford each month for: housing? food? savings?			

In order for your plan to work, you also need to know your personal net worth. That's the difference between your assets (things you own) and your liabilities (money you owe). Include in assets your home, automobiles, personal property, value of your own business, savings account, and other assets, and compare the total value to your debts. The difference is net worth. It's important to identify net worth because your plan should include goals for protecting what you have now (meaning you won't want to spend assets, but preserve them). And you will ultimately increase net worth by getting out of debt. Tracking your net worth is an excellent way to judge the success of short-term and long-term goals.

One sensitive spot in many families is the question of who should control the money. Debt problems might arise over this issue in the first place. If both of you think you should be in control, then each will pursue spending habits and priorities individually. There's no coordinated plan and absolutely no agreement on goals.

How do you reconcile this problem? The solution is to agree to share responsibility. Bills can be paid jointly and it really doesn't matter who makes out the checks. The important question is, "What's the repayment schedule?" As long as you work from this plan and within your budget, the question of control doesn't matter. Control should rest in the budget and agreed-upon goals and not in the hands of one spouse or the other.

A lot of disagreement comes from holding conflicting ideas about what your family can afford. We listed four items: debt payments, housing, food, and savings. There is a lot more than this, of course. But raising the question at least points out the big differences in perception between you and your spouse.

Once you write your answers on the goal worksheet and look at the differences, you can begin narrowing down the areas of conflict. Ultimately, you will be on the same path to eliminating debts, and you will agree on your long-term goals and rules for spending money.

MAKING THE GOAL VISUAL

Having a goal and being able to see progress each and every month is a reassuring and satisfying experience. You can ensure that you stay on schedule by making your goals as visual as possible. Put the goal on a chart and track it each month. The purpose: To make sure your progress stays at or ahead of the schedule.

Example: Your goal is to repay current debts according to the schedule you built. You construct a chart and show the goal with a broken line. Each month, as you make the scheduled payments, you track progress with a solid line. As long as the solid line is at or above the broken line, you're on track; you're reaching your goal.

A chart should show the steps of your goal from top to bottom, and the time schedule from left to right. Figure 2–5 shows how this is done.

How does the goal chart help? There are a number of benefits in making your goals visual:

1. It lets you *see* progress as you make it. That's a rewarding experience that builds confidence and lets you believe in your accomplishments.

2. It acts as an early warning system. If your solid line falls below the broken line, you will need to identify why that happened and take steps to get the progress line back where it belongs—before the problem gets out of hand.

3. It puts you in the habit of setting and tracking goals. That's how you achieve success. You will reach the goals you set as long as you follow them and watch out for trouble along the way.

A goal chart can be built for any goal you set, whether short term or long term. Some examples:

- Your goal is to repay current debts over the next 12 months. The total amount of debt is listed from top to bottom (on the top is the total you owe, on the bottom is zero). Progress is measured by the amount of debt you have repaid each month. The 12 months are listed from left to right.

FIGURE 2–5
Goal Chart

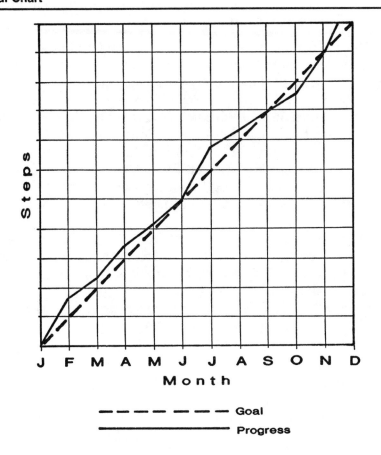

- Your goal is to save $20,000 for a down payment on a home. You plan to accomplish this within 24 months. Current savings are $12,000, so you need to save $333 per month. List 24 segments from top to bottom, each one representing $333, and list the 24 months from left to right.
- Your goal is to put at least $50 per month into savings. Each step (top to bottom) has a value of $50, and months are listed from left to right. As long as you put at least $50 in savings each month, the progress line will be at or

above the goal line. If you don't make the full payment one month, you can see that it needs to be made up the following month to stay on track.

Once you have your priorities in order for short-term and for long-term goals, the desired result is clearly understood. And in the process of defining your goals, you have also defined the problem. That's what the repayment schedule reveals.

The definition phase is over. It's all subject to change once you get into the budgeting process. Many families have tried budgeting, only to fail. They found it difficult or impossible to follow for one reason: They just listed what they had to pay each month, without taking the other steps: defining the problem, setting goals, and making sensible rules to control spending habits.

A budget works when it's put into action *after* taking the steps we've described in this chapter. Without agreeing with your spouse on definition of the problem and the goals, and without setting rules for getting rid of the problem, the budget simply won't work. The next chapter shows you how to create a family budget that really works, that you'll be able to follow, and that you can use to reach your short-term and long-term goals.

CHAPTER 3

A PENNY HERE,
A PENNY THERE

Money is always there but
the pockets change.
—*Gertrude Stein*

Children are given a very limited allowance, but adults have all the money they want. At least that's what many of us grew up believing. And because we equate the freedom to spend with being grown up, we resist the idea of having to live within a confining budget. That's why most attempts at budgeting fail. A budget is a limit on what we can do—a restrictive allowance. If you try to take charge of your money by carefully counting every penny, then you will miss the whole point of budgeting. The exercise should not be undertaken to limit what you can do in the way that parents limit their children's spending habits. Instead, a budget can and should be a planning tool, an estimate of the immediate future.

AVOIDING THE FIVE COMMON MISTAKES

There are five mistakes worth avoiding when you attempt to set up a family budget. They are:

1. Thinking of the Budget in Absolute Terms

You might resist the idea of setting up a budget because that feels like the ultimate loss of freedom. If you must account for every penny and if the budget rules how much you can spend each day, then it's a punitive measure rather than a helpful tool for managing and planning money.

The budget you establish for yourself will help you to plan ahead, even if planning only means making it from one paycheck to another. For example, you know that a big insurance premium is coming due next month. By budgeting for it now, you will not be caught by surprise and forced to go further into debt to survive to the next paycheck. That's the kind of value you want to look for in the budgeting process.

2. Setting Too Strict a Budget

Solutions don't come from extreme action, but from methodical, gradual change. The budget should not be thought of as a fix-all that demands superhuman discipline. If you establish a budget that will account for every penny and robs you of all of life's pleasures, you're being too tough on yourself.

Forget the notion that the budget exists to police your spending habits. Of all the misconceptions about managing debt, the worst one is that budgets must succeed each and every month, or *you* have failed. Relax. The budget is your tool. You're in command. The only real failure is in not even trying to solve your debt problem.

3. Forcing Budgetary Restrictions on Yourself

Remember, the budget is an estimate of what you will spend in the next week or two, or in the next month. The budget cannot possibly go beyond the immediate future, because everything will change within the next two to three months. Budgeting is a process of planning, best used to get you from one paycheck to another, to anticipate the near future and plan for it today, and to help you regain control.

All too often, families establish budgets for themselves and fall into the trap of trying to live strictly by that budget. They give up the occasional dinner or movie because they've left no provision for that expense. They no longer take a day trip to the country because they're already at their budget's limit for auto expenses. And they put off buying new shoes because their clothing allowance isn't big enough.

To get out of debt, you will need to plan and control your money carefully. That doesn't mean having to give up every small pleasure or delay necessities. If you place too many restrictions on yourself, your budget will probably fail.

4. Believing You're Failing Where Everyone Else Is Succeeding

Everyone who tries to budget their money runs into problems. There's really no failure in running over your budget, and doing so doesn't mean you lack the discipline to control your money. It only means that your budget wasn't planned well enough, and that you ran into expenses you didn't foresee. Budgeting isn't easy for anyone. You're not alone.

When you do spend more than you estimated, you have the information to improve your next budget. Learning from mistakes is real success, and you can only succeed by improving. So think of the budget overrun as part of the process, and not as a sign that you just can't take charge. By establishing a budget and making your best effort, you're already on the way to taking command of your financial affairs.

5. Going Too Far in Tracking Expenses

You have probably heard that the first step in taking charge of your money is figuring out exactly where you're spending it. The theory is that if you write down every penny you spend, you'll somehow find the key to control. But that means that each time you buy a candy bar or a newspaper, you have to jot down the expense in a notebook.

Obsessive accounting doesn't serve any useful purpose. It only makes you a slave to money and adds to the sense of guilt and failure that prevents you from working with a budget and eventually getting out of debt. Few people know where they spend all of their money; it's a mystery to them. But writing down every cent you spend isn't the solution. Once you have a realistic budget, you'll be able to compare your plan to actual expenses. If the budget isn't working, you have a choice: change spending patterns or change the budget.

Set a standard for yourself for each category of expense, and then track actual expenses against the standard. That's where budgeting becomes truly valuable. This will help you to identify areas where you can cut expenses or where your spending habits can be modified.

SETTING UP THE BUDGET

Your first step in establishing an effective, working budget is to list all of the categories of expense you face each month. Your purpose is to estimate ahead of time how much you will spend. This plan will be valuable when you review actual results later.

Example: One of your categories is lunch expense. You commute to work each day and buy your lunch. When you first think about this expense, you estimate that $50 or $60 will cover it. But you soon discover that, in fact, you're spending closer to $200 every month.

By comparing the budget to actual expenses, you discover one spending problem. But there's a solution. Either you must increase your budget for what you're really spending on lunches, or you will have to change the spending pattern. If you increase the budget for lunches, the budget for some other expense will have to be decreased, and that's not always possible.

The solution might be to alternate between buying lunches and packing your own lunch. Once you decide what you can really afford, the realistic way to cut down on the expense will become obvious.

In this example, budgeting was used in the best possible way. Instead of placing an impossible limit (thus ensuring failure), it brought a specific problem to the surface and led to realistic alternatives. The solution can only be decided once the scope of the problem has been defined, and that's what proper use of the budget allows you to do.

Your budget doesn't have to be formal or complex, and it certainly cannot be permanent. Your income changes over time, and so do your expenses. Budgets should be set up for the next two to three pay periods. For example, if you're paid twice per month, set up today's budget for the next three pay periods. Modify the budget each time you're paid, based on:

- How the previous budget turns out.
- New expenses that come up.

If the previous budget falls short, immediately look for ways to prevent that from happening again—even if you can't completely eliminate the problem, but can only reduce the amount by which you fall short. Set a goal for yourself:

> *Some degree of progress will be made*
> *with each new budget.*

The progress may be very small. Even if you improve your financial condition by only a few dollars, that's a start. And it's better than making no progress at all or sinking further into debt.

Some examples of progress:

- Reducing the amount of debt on a loan or credit card account.
- Doing away with an unnecessarily high expense.
- Putting the budgeted amount of money into savings.

The expense plan, which will run two to three pay periods into the future, is an estimate of what you will spend in each budget category. An example of this worksheet is shown in Figure 3–1.

Remember, this worksheet does not represent the restrictions you will place on yourself. It's only an estimate of how you will spend your money. Some categories, like auto repairs and medical expenses, will have to be estimated. You might run above or below the levels you set up in the budget.

This worksheet will prove a valuable exercise in planning and controlling your spending habits. It helps you make an important change: thinking ahead *before* going out and spending money, thus avoiding future problems.

We mentioned in the emergency plan that one important step is to avoid future debt. That's essential, especially when

FIGURE 3–1
Expense Plan

Expense Plan

DESCRIPTION	PAYMENT DATE		
Savings			
Food			
Rent			
Telephone			
Utilities			
Auto Gas			
Auto Repairs			
Insurance			
Clothing			
Medical			
Laundry			
Subscriptions and Dues			
Entertainment			
Commuting			
Loan Payments			
_____			
_____			
_____			
Credit Card Payments			
_____			
_____			
Store Accounts			
_____			
_____			
Other			
_____			
_____			
_____			
Total			

you are still in the emergency phase of your plan to get out of debt. But in some cases, you might want to make a purchase that will require going into debt which might be acceptable. You may set rules for yourself.

For example, let's say you visit a computer store and you see a computer you want to buy. Without a budget, you might just buy it on the spot, figuring the small monthly payment on your credit card won't hurt too much. As you know, doing that a few times adds up to a big debt problem. Now, with a budget, you're aware of the need to make progress with each budgeting period—even a little progress. So if you want that computer, it will require some planning.

Instead of spending money impulsively or justifying an increased debt level, you have a plan. You can set aside part of your budget for that computer. Putting only a few extra dollars into savings each month might mean you'll have to wait quite a while until you can get it. You might also plan the budget so that you do go into debt for the computer—but only when you can afford to repay more debt than you add each month. You probably have set up provisions in your budget to repay other outstanding debts. If you now go further into debt to buy a computer, your budget should have enough room to increase your overall debt repayments so that the level of *total* debt is reduced each month.

This guideline places a limit on the amount of new debt you can incur. It's not realistic to set the rule that you'll never go into debt again. Instead, you can control and plan debt levels so that you're in control. It is possible to add debts and, at the same time, make progress in your monthly budget.

LIVING WITHIN THE BUDGET

Everyone knows how hard it is to live within their budget. And of course, this idea comes from the theory that a budget is a restriction on what you can spend, and on how you can live.

Let's redefine living within the budget to mean you will begin to operate with these standards:

- You will plan ahead for upcoming expense commitments.
- You will compare actual to budget each period, and look for ways to improve.
- You will modify spending habits so that future spending levels won't take you by surprise.
- You will make some progress in each and every budget.

The example of buying a computer is applicable to each of these rules. Just because you have a budget doesn't mean you can no longer go out and buy the things you want now and then, nor does it mean that you will have to wait many months—even years—before you'll be able to spend freely. A budget that requires sacrifice and delay for the indefinite future isn't the answer.

You can *plan ahead* for the computer by making room in your budget, either by putting extra money in savings or planning and controlling additional debt.

You *compare actual to budget* to find ways to afford the computer you want. As your planning process begins to work, you will free up funds so that you can truly afford the computer with the debt you incur to buy it now.

You will *modify spending habits* because you're working from a plan. The computer purchase won't be made impulsively, but as part of your budget.

You will *make progress* by working the purchase into your budget. That means the money will be there to continue paying off other debts; in addition, you will have a precise date in mind for elimination of the new debt.

We have given an example of going into debt to buy a new computer that you probably don't really need. But there is a significant difference between taking that action with a budget and just spending money.

The process of getting out of debt is too often based on the premise that you *must* stop incurring new debt. This might be possible for some people. But the important change comes about when you plan your future finances rather than constantly struggle with them; when your debts continue to rise, no matter what you try; and when you just can't find an answer to the growing debt problems you face.

You can afford the luxury of not waiting, as long as you have gained enough control over your budget that buying a computer (or any other nonessential) is feasible. If you're in a severe debt crunch, you obviously need to gain control before you can afford to incur more debt. And your purpose should be to control debt levels, and not necessarily to completely avoid debt in the future.

There is nothing wrong with taking on a temporary debt, as long as your plan proves that you can afford repayments—without draining your savings, forcing you to cut back on food and other necessities, delaying progress in repaying other debts, or otherwise harming your financial condition.

GOALS AND ACTION STEPS

With a budget you have control within your grasp. You will use the budgeting process to plan the future and, just as critically, to take corrective action when actual expenses run over the budget.

It's self-defeating to set up an unrealistic budget and to then berate yourself when it fails. A much more constructive use of the budget is to focus it on the areas that you can improve, and to then take action. In order to do this, you will need to compare actual and budgeted expenses for each period and examine those expenses that ran over. Coordinating this effort by pay period is the most practical for most people, because you will be able to match income with spending.

To isolate what you actually spend in any one category, you will have to figure out a way to keep track. This is one reason some people suggest writing down every penny you spend. But there's an easier way.

During each pay period, you will pay most of your bills by check. Some expenses, though, require cash. The allowance you and your spouse take for lunches, entertainment, and incidentals, are the categories where many problems occur. Most families deposit their checks and take out the cash they need for the coming two weeks or half month. The way to keep track of expenses is to assign specific amounts of money to each budget category. For example, your daily lunch expenses are budgeted at $100, and you're paid twice per month. So for each pay period, you'll take $50 just for lunches.

Some important rules to follow in order to keep track:

1. If you use any of the funds for reasons other than the budgeted category, replace those funds.

2. If you run out of money and cash a check for more, make a note of it. You don't have to keep track of every cent, just the round amounts you take out.

3. Take just the amount allowed for in the budget, even if you think you'll run out before the end of the pay period.

As you can see, you can track broad categories of cash expenses without having to account for every penny you spend. At the end of the pay period, compare your goal (the budgeted amount) to what you actually spent. Then decide what actions you need to take to avoid problems in the next budgeting period.

Fill out a worksheet like the one shown in Figure 3–2. This should be used only for those budget categories in which you ran over the amount set aside.

This is not just an exercise in recording budget problems and then increasing the budget. That's a passive response to a discovered problem. The action steps can take many forms, but it's critical that you list the problem areas and then consider alternatives. Some examples:

- Your expense for lunches during one half-month period ran over the budget by $40. Your choices: increase the budget, cut back on lunch expenses, or compromise by taking a lunch to work two or three times each week.
- You set aside $100 for entertainment last month, but you ended up spending $250. You may want to cut back on the extras for now, or meet in the middle: cut back moderately and increase the budget somewhat. But remember, when you increase your budget in one area, you reduce it somewhere else.
- Your budget for food during a two-week period was $250, but you spent nearly $400. You look over the payment record, and discover that most of the problem occurs during the week, when you make several trips in between

FIGURE 3–2
Expense Goals

Expense Goals

Month _____

DESCRIPTION	GOAL	ACTUAL	OVER

ACTION STEPS

_____

_____

_____

_____

_____

_____

_____

_____

_____

the weekly major shopping. The solution: continue the once-per-week major trip, and limit other food expenses to the necessities. Shop only from a list, and don't buy anything not on that list.

Taking action is essential. Budgeting is a series of goals expressed financially. But they only work if you follow up on what you discover, by correcting problems in the budget itself (inadequate amounts set aside), and in your spending habits (impulsive and nonessential buying).

SHORT-TERM GOALS

The budget is a mechanism for getting from one period to another, with specific planning incorporated into it. But beyond that, the budget also helps you put short-term goals into action.

Example: You have decided to eliminate credit card debt within one year. To do so, your budget includes payments each period to retire those balances. The rules you set for yourself are:

- The credit cards won't be used again until the entire balances have been repaid.
- Once the current balance is gone, the cards will only be used to the extent that the entire balance can be paid off every month.

Another short-term goal might be to start a savings account and deposit money into it each pay period—without exception. So you set that goal and corresponding rules for yourself:

- The savings deposit will be made at the beginning of each pay period.
- Savings won't be withdrawn except for extreme emergencies.

Setting short-term goals helps you prevent the cycle of debt you've experienced in the past. Looking at the whole problem is overwhelming and depressing, but by using a budget for the next half month, all you need to do is set a few goals:

- I will make some progress every period.
- I will follow up on discovered problems and resolve them.
- I will not incur any additional spending unless the budget allows for it.

REVISING THE REPAYMENT SCHEDULE

In the last chapter, we introduced the idea of devising a repayment schedule; and then revising that schedule based on what your budget reveals. Your plan to eliminate debt, set up a savings account, and avoid going further into debt in the future might be impossible based on the volume of repayments. A revision should be undertaken once you compare available income to monthly commitments.

Example: You want to save some money every month and still make progress in eliminating debts. But the minimum monthly repayment of your collective debts won't allow you to budget even for the necessities, not to mention saving part of your paycheck.

Now that you have defined the scope of your problem, it's time to modify your repayment schedule. If your existing debts are so large that you can't afford to keep up with the desirable schedule, take these steps:

1. Figure out what you can afford, keeping in mind the need to pay *more* than the monthly interest your creditors are charging. (Otherwise, the debt keeps getting larger, even when you make payments.)
2. Revise your budget with the new payment schedule in mind. Make certain that the plan is realistic and that you have enough flexibility in your budget to afford the proposed level of payments.
3. Contact each creditor. Explain the problem and make a commitment: to repay all that you owe, and to not miss any payments.
4. Put the revised plan into effect.
5. Stick to the commitment.

You may also ask creditors to suspend interest charges. Some will agree to this, while others will not. Some creditors may even reject your proposed revision and insist on payment of the minimum amount. Some points to make concerning this problem:

- You may put your plan into effect, even if the creditor doesn't agree to it. Most creditors will accept your payment, even if it's very small, rather than get nothing at all.
- In most cases, as long as you continue making payments, and as long as the creditor accepts those payments, you will be allowed to continue with your plan.
- You can always appeal to reason. If your debts are simply too high to manage the required minimum payment on your income, the creditor's choice might come down to getting everything owed over a longer period of time; or getting nothing at all.

THE LONG-TERM PLAN

During the first few months or years that you're operating with a budget, you may have to concentrate on building very slowly. You may be putting only a few dollars into savings and seeing debts decline very, very slowly. But even a slow pace of improvement is better than continuing to live under the cloud of ever-growing debt.

Eventually, though, you will gain enough control that you will have some flexibility in your budget. You will be able to apply part of a salary increase to accelerating debt repayments and even to increasing your monthly savings. At that point, you will want to start thinking about long-term goals.

You can work long-term goals into the budget you use from one pay period to the next. For example, if you want to save for a child's college education, put some money into a retirement fund, or invest in a mutual fund or annuity, your budget is a perfect control tool for those goals.

Example: You have eliminated a large portion of your previous debt, and recently you were given a raise. You suddenly have flexibility in your budget.

At this point, the impulse is to relax diligence and spend more money every month. Because you have more room in the budget, it's easy to revert to the destructive debt cycle you experienced before. But now, with more income, you face the danger of incurring an even higher level of debt—repeating past mistakes on a larger scale.

The solution is to continue monthly budgeting with long-term goals in mind. Use some of the extra money to reward yourself with entertainment, hobby, and leisure activities. But also increase the amount you put into savings. At the same time, continue to avoid incurring debts you cannot manage. Finally, decide how to reach your long-term goals on your budget. Put some money into a separate savings account or begin an investment program designed with those goals in mind.

If you understand why the traditional, restrictive budget fails, you can avoid repeating problems from the past. The budget is a planning tool, a general guideline for development of an attitude toward timing of expenses and control of funds. But even with the best plan, the whole process can be thrown into confusion by unexpected expenses—medical bills, car repairs, and maintenance of your home. You can prepare for these unexpected problems by using the budget wisely and anticipating future expenses by setting aside extra money every pay period. That action helps you avoid future unplanned debt and helps your budget work. Unexpected expense strategies are explained in the next chapter.

CHAPTER 4

THOSE UNEXPECTED
SURPRISES

Driving 'round a bend and skidding
on a mat of dead toads is very
unpleasant for all concerned.
—*Amanda Hillier*

Budgeting would be an easy task if you always knew well in advance exactly what expenses were coming up. The real challenge in budgeting is not in scheduling the known expense; it's in being able to anticipate what's coming up in the next month.

Example: You have created a detailed monthly budget, and you're able to stick with it consistently. But three months after you start the process, several things happen. You get a bill from your insurance company for one year's premium; your car breaks down; you have to call a plumber; your union dues have to be paid; and it's time to buy your children clothing for the school year that's about to start.

If your budget didn't allow for these expenses, that doesn't mean it failed. But it does mean you overlooked some expenses, and that some other expenses came up that you couldn't plan for in advance.

The unexpected is always the most difficult problem in your family budget. Some spending problems can be controlled, of course. You will have a budgeting problem if you spend more than you can afford on optional things, like entertainment, luxuries, or hobbies. And if you go into debt before getting rid of the debt balances you already owe, you'll be unable to take control. But assuming that you are making a sincere effort to get the upper hand, you still need to deal with two groups of troublesome expenses that aren't always planned for in advance: variable bills and unexpected bills.

These two groups create most of the budgeting problems you will encounter each month, more so than the problem of overspending in a known category. You will need to plan well ahead each month, and improve your management skills by comparing the budget to actual expenses. But beyond that, you'll also need to look ahead as far as a year so that you won't be taken by surprise.

Planning helps you avoid the common problem of having to continue incurring debt, even when you are determined to avoid debt in the future. By setting aside a reserve for variable and unexpected future bills, you'll have the money to pay them, and you won't have to make one of the other three choices: borrowing more money, delaying payment of the unexpected bill, or delaying repayment of other debts. All three of these alternatives only defeat your goal of getting out of debt and staying there.

Example: A family has brought its monthly budget under control. They're managing expenses, scheduling repayment of debts, and making real progress. But when they get an unexpected bill, they conclude that budgeting simply doesn't work. They can't possibly know when bills for car repairs, home maintenance, and other unknowns will come up, so what's the point? Their well-conceived budget is abandoned.

In this example, the budget did not fail. It was working, but it didn't go far enough. It didn't allow for the expenses that came up other than on a monthly basis, or for the contingencies that always seem to pop up at the worst possible times. Instead of abandoning the budget, it should be taken one additional step.

Unexpected and variable bills defeat a good number of savings plans that people make. It seems impossible to put money away every month, when each month seems to come with a crisis of its own that just wasn't expected. In that situation, savings are the only immediate source for relief, or so it might seem.

Example: You have been putting $50 per month into a savings account for the last year and haven't touched it. You have $600, plus interest. But an unexpected medical bill comes up for something not covered by your insurance plan. You need $500, and the only place you can get it is from your savings account.

You can solve the difficult problem of variable and unexpected bills by setting aside a reserve each month. This reserve is intended just for those bills that don't fit into a regular, monthly budget. The reserve is also separate from your savings account.

The reserve money can be put into the same account as your more permanent savings, if that's convenient. Or you can use a money market fund or a separate account for your reserve. And your savings can be used for extreme emergencies; that's one purpose of having the savings account. We're concerned here not with the emergency—losing your job, unexpected illness, or necessary repairs to your house—but with the routine, recurring expenses everyone experiences that are difficult to time.

PLANNING FOR THE VARIABLES

A variable bill is one that doesn't recur every month. Some expenses (often the larger ones) are due every three months, or even twice each year. Some examples:

- Insurance premiums that are paid quarterly, semi-annually, or annually.
- Property tax bills due twice per year.
- Income tax prepayments.
- Subscriptions and dues.
- Clothing expenses (for example, a wardrobe for your child at the beginning of the school year).
- Christmas shopping.

You know about these expenses, so they can be planned, predicted, and scheduled. The problems you're likely to encounter come up because you didn't plan well enough, or look far enough ahead. Variable bills will take you by surprise if you don't plan for them; and chances are, you'll have a lot of variables, all coming due within one or two months. That can throw your budget into chaos.

By creating a reserve for known variable expenses, and budgeting for that reserve each month, you will remove pressure from your budget. For example, you know that a $400 bill is coming due in four months. You need to set aside $100 per month—as part of your budget—so that you'll have the money on hand when the bill comes in.

Start by listing *all* of your known expenses. Arrange them by groupings based on frequency of payment. For example, your monthly expenses can be summarized first:

Food	$ 500
Mortgage	425
All other	400
Total	$1,325

As part of the "all other" group, let's assume you have budgeted a set monthly amount for savings. This should be considered as separate from any reserve you put aside for future expenses. Think of savings not as available money to be used for those inconvenient expenses that come up unexpectedly, but as money put aside to be kept and built up.

In addition to your recurring monthly expenses, you also have expenses that are paid each quarter. Union dues are paid in January, April, July, and October; and life insurance premiums are paid in March, June, September, and December:

Union dues	$107
Life insurance	410
Total	$517

You also pay your property taxes on your own, instead of allowing your lender to collect a portion of the total bill each month. You usually have that choice, and it may be wiser to set aside your own reserve and earn interest, rather than letting your lender use your money for as long as six months. These taxes are due twice each year, in April and October. Each payment is $280.

With all known fixed and variable expenses in mind, you can now prepare your full-year budget:

Monthly Budget

Month	Monthly Expenses	Quarterly Expenses	Semi-Annual Expenses	Total
January	$ 1,325	$ 107	—	$ 1,432
February	1,325	—	—	1,325
March	1,325	410	—	1,735
April	1,325	107	280	1,712
May	1,325	—	—	1,325
June	1,325	410	—	1,735
July	1,325	107	—	1,432
August	1,325	—	—	1,325
September	1,325	410	—	1,735
October	1,325	107	280	1,712
November	1,325	—	—	1,325
December	1,325	410	—	1,735
Total	$15,900	$2,068	$560	$18,528
Average				$ 1,544

This one-year plan identifies the average monthly expense level, which is more important than the monthly amount. Many people have trouble with their budgets because they estimate expenses based only on the monthly. For example, you might believe your "average" monthly expenses are $1,325, based on the example above. But in fact, the true average is $1,544. That's what you need to have each month throughout the year, just to meet known expenses. If you base your budget only on the monthly level, you'll be off by an average of more than $200 per month.

Unless you include an allowance for variable expenses, you will be taken by surprise constantly. You'll notice that when variable expenses hit your budget, the required levels for those months are substantially higher than the average. When above-average expense levels occur two months in a row, your monthly budget could be in big trouble. In the example, this happens in March/April and in September/October.

You can identify the true monthly average by preparing a schedule that includes variable expenses. Your monthly budget should be based on the average expense so that you won't run into problems when variable bills show up. Your budget then calls for setting aside the true average, rather than just what you need for the next 30 days. This is a fairly easy planning task. You know about the variables, and can schedule them a full year in advance.

PLANNING FOR THE UNEXPECTED

Unexpected bills pose a different problem. You don't know the amount of bills in the immediate future, and you have no way of knowing when they'll come up. The way to plan for unexpected bills is to come up with an estimate based on the previous 12 months.

Estimates cannot be dependable. By their nature they are nothing more than a best guess. But when it comes to budgeting, your task is to plan with the information you have and to try and anticipate those bills you are likely to have. We all set patterns in our lives, and those patterns are often seen in the nature of unexpected expenses. For example, you can use the past to estimate the frequency of auto repairs, medical expenses, and home maintenance.

To estimate unexpected expenses, go through your checkbook for the previous year and make a list of unexpected expenses you paid each month. Use that to develop an estimate of what you might have in the coming year. While the past doesn't tell you what will happen in the future, it's the best information available to you.

Example: You know your fixed monthly expenses are $1,325, and you also know your quarterly and semi-annual variable expenses. Now you need to estimate the unknown elements of your budget. You go through last year's checkbook and prepare this list:

Unexpected Expenses

January	Medical	$ 307
February	Medical	195
March	Plumber	180
April	Speeding ticket	75
May	Car repair	415
June	—	0
July	Medical	316
August	Plumber	145
September	Car repair	290
October	—	0
November	—	0
December	Christmas	412
Total		$2,335
Average		$ 195

Based on the previous year's record, you know you are likely to have an average of $200 per month in unexpected expenses. The next year will involve an entirely different experience; but remember, this is only your best guess. The next step is to bring the average monthly allowance for unexpected expenses into your budget.

Example: In the summary of expenses, we came up with a monthly average of $1,544. Based on historical levels, you decide to add $200 per month for unexpected expenses. Now you know it will be necessary to set aside $1,744 every month to pay for all known expenses and for what you estimate you'll have to pay for the unexpected. The monthly average developed in the previous example must be increased by $200 to include a reserve for unexpected expenses. Actual monthly expenses vary quite a bit each month. This variation is shown in Figure 4–1.

The purpose of setting aside reserves is to stabilize your monthly budget. When you know how much must be put aside, either to pay current bills or to save for the variable and unexpected bills in the near future, you will be able to maintain savings and reduce debt. The alternative is to not budget at all and face each month as it comes up. And that's not acceptable if you want to take control of your financial life.

Make a distinction between reserves for upcoming expenses and savings. In the fixed monthly budget, we identified

FIGURE 4–1
Monthly Expense Levels

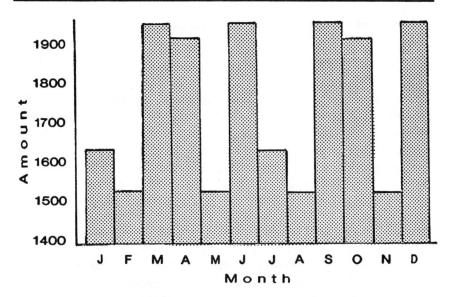

amounts for food, mortgage, and all other. Included in the "all other" category should be a fixed amount you'll put in savings each month.

By combining a monthly budget for savings with the reserve for variable and unexpected expenses, you should be able to achieve three purposes in your budget:

1. Debt Reduction

Your budget should be used to plan for the gradual elimination of all existing debts. Your standard: to eliminate all debts before incurring any additional credit card balances or loans. By using the reserve method, you will be able to continue your debt reduction plan without needing to incur more debt.

2. Savings Accumulation

Savings should be a fixed, permanent part of your budget. The same amount is put into your savings account each and every month, to be used for long-term goals only. The exception: Savings may have to be used to pay for exceptionally large, unexpected expenses that are higher than the reserve you've set aside and that can't be delayed.

3. Budget Control

The fixed, monthly expense is only part of the total budget. By establishing reserves, you will equalize the monthly budget burden. This lets you continue to build your savings account while reducing your debt level each and every month; and at the same time, you can deal with the surprises that do come up.

SPENDING THE RESERVE

Reserves are created to even out the level of monthly expense, even when your actual budget varies considerably from one month to the next. Reserves are a cushion. You will need to plan the reserve so that monthly payments are spread evenly. Some payments in some months will go into your reserve, and in other months, exceptionally high payments will be made, meaning that the reserve balance must be reduced.

The table below shows how this works. The amount set aside each month (budget) is your average monthly requirement. The amount spent each month (expenses) is your expense commitment level. And the last column (balance) shows how much is left in your reserve at the end of the month. (The balance at the end of April and October is in the red, but the amount is so small that it shouldn't be a problem. You can delay some payments by a week and pick up the difference in the next month.)

The relationship between reserves and expense levels is illustrated in Figure 4–2. Note that the reserve balance is above the "zero" line most of the year and that it dips slightly below that line only twice. Using this method, you will be able to predict upcoming expenses and avoid unpleasant budget surprises.

Reserve Planning

Month	Budget	Expenses	Balance
January	$1,744	$1,632	$ 112
February	1,744	1,525	331
March	1,744	1,935	140
April	1,744	1,912	− 28
May	1,744	1,525	191
June	1,744	1,935	0
July	1,744	1,632	112
August	1,744	1,525	331
September	1,744	1,935	140
October	1,744	1,912	− 28
November	1,744	1,525	191
December	1,744	1,935	0

FIGURE 4–2
Expenses and Reserves

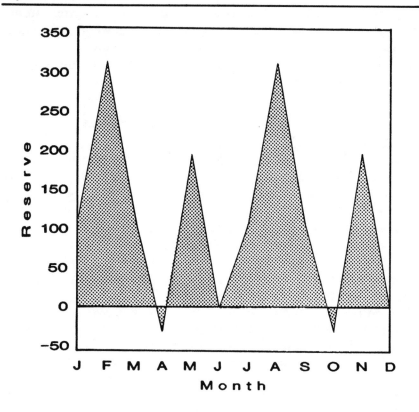

WHERE TO KEEP THE RESERVE

Having extra money around, even when you know you'll need it next month, can be very tempting. Even a local savings account might prove difficult to maintain, because the money is so accessible. Since it's desirable to keep savings and reserve separate, how can you handle the reserve money efficiently? You have several choices:

1. Put Reserve Money into Savings

You may deposit your reserve balance into your existing savings account and withdraw it later when expenses come up. The advantage of this is that you will earn interest on extra balances. If unexpected expenses don't come up as often as you anticipate, your reserve will grow and earn interest and might not even be needed. The disadvantage is that, by combining savings and reserves, it is easier to use savings when you would rather leave those funds intact. In addition, you will have to withdraw or transfer funds from savings to checking several times each year.

2. Leave the Money in Your Checking Account

If you are able to exercise a lot of control, you can simply leave reserve funds in your checking account and use them only when variable and unexpected expenses occur. This may be the most convenient choice, but it may also be too easy to just write checks. When your balance is temporarily higher than average, there may be a tendency to spend carelessly. In some cases, it's better to remove the funds.

Another choice is to leave reserve funds in your checking account, but not include them in your balance. That may reduce the temptation to spend too much, but it also complicates the task of balancing your checking account each month. If you do leave reserve funds in your checking account, be sure your bank pays interest on those balances each month.

3. Set Up a Separate Savings Account

Another idea is to set up a separate savings account, just for your reserve balances. In this way, the funds are separated and will earn interest. But you must still withdraw or transfer the money you need each month to pay variable and unexpected expenses.

4. Open a Money Market Fund or Account

You can also deposit reserve funds in a money market mutual fund or in a similar account offered by your bank. In these funds and accounts, money is pooled and invested in short-term money instruments of the U.S. government and corporations. You can get your money back easily, usually just by writing a check to yourself. Most funds and accounts require a minimum check amount, usually $250 or $500.

5. Keep It in Cash

You can also keep reserve funds in cash, hidden away for future use. While this does remove the balances from other checking or savings accounts, it also poses several problems. First, keeping cash in your house is not a wise idea. Second, you give up interest on what could become considerable balances. Third, cash is just as tempting to spend as checking account balances. And fourth, when you need some of the reserve, you still need to make a deposit to your checking account before writing checks. This is the least practical alternative.

You should keep your money in interest-bearing accounts, especially when dealing with reserve balances you won't need for a month or more. But you will also need to set goals for yourself, including the rule that you will not use reserve funds for any purpose other than those you establish in your budget.

RUNNING OUT OF MONEY

Everyone knows what it's like not to have enough money to pay all of their expenses or to buy the things they'd like. In some cases, even necessities are delayed because, as the saying goes, "I ran out of money before I ran out of month."

Budgeting for variable and unexpected expenses does not have to be exact, and it doesn't have to be put into action at 100 percent. If you can plan for *most* of the variable and unexpected expenses you'll encounter, that's progress. If you can avoid going further into debt most of the time, you at least reduce the continuing debt problem. And if you can set aside a reserve that makes your monthly budget work a little better, you're gradually overcoming the debt syndrome.

Just as budgeting itself should not be an absolute process in which you succeed or fail, expense planning takes place gradually. Debts are eliminated a little at a time. Expenses are brought under control, your plan starts to work, and surprises don't come up as often.

Don't be overly critical of yourself if you overlook a variable expense or budget too little for unexpected expenses. The important action is to begin the process of control. As you exercise that process, you will improve and begin to gain ever-growing levels of financial management.

Example: You know that you will spend several hundred dollars at the end of the year for Christmas. But your budget simply isn't flexible enough to put money aside for those expenses. So when the Christmas season comes, you use credit cards to buy gifts.

This shortfall might be considered a setback, a failure in the budgeting process. But in fact, it's simply reality. You haven't failed, you've only identified one problem in the monthly budgeting. You will overcome it with several steps:

1. Save half of the Christmas budget next year. That's better than saving nothing at all, and it will reduce the additional debt you'll incur next year.
2. Schedule credit card payments in next year's budget. Set a goal to pay off the balances within a few months.

3. Avoid using your credit cards next year. By cutting off the debt cycle, you will put a cap on the level of continuing debt.
4. Keep putting money into savings. Don't deplete your savings account to pay for expenses. Even though you'll have to pay interest on your credit card balances, you will want to preserve savings and keep those balances separate from your monthly expenses. If you attempt to solve the expense problem by spending assets rather than income, you will take a step backward—an action you want to avoid.

Budgets serve a purpose beyond expense planning. If used properly, they also help you avoid future debt. You may put a lot of effort into gaining control over spending habits, trying to keep debt balances low, and paying off old balances, only to find yourself slipping further into debt.

In that situation, the budget is a valuable tool for identifying problem areas, gaining control, and keeping it. When expenses come up unexpectedly and you don't have a reserve set aside, the only obvious choices are to dip into savings, or to use credit cards or other lines of credit.

Managing expenses with debt is a self-defeating process because it keeps you in debt. You end up paying interest with money that could be used to accumulate net worth; and you never have enough cash on hand because so much of your budget has to go into making minimum payments on credit card accounts, or making scheduled payments on bank loans.

PLANNING A YEAR IN ADVANCE

The budget—as a device for estimating and planning for the future—will never anticipate every expense you're likely to have. Planning can help only so much. But by exercising the management techniques for variable and unexpected expenses, you will make the best possible use of the budgeting process.

Some additional suggestions:

1. Don't Use Debt to Solve Budget Problems

Overcoming this month's debt problems by going into more debt doesn't solve anything; it only makes the problem worse. It's easy to fall into this trap. An unexpected bill comes up, and you can't delay it. So you pay for it with your credit card, borrow money, or delay repayments of other debts.

The solution: Begin using the reserve method to anticipate variable expenses and to put money aside for unexpected expenses. You might not be able to set up a fully reserved procedure immediately, because current debt payments don't leave room for any reserve at all. Give yourself a few months to get the new system in place gradually, even if you can only afford to set up a minimum reserve at first.

2. Constantly Adjust Reserve Requirements

The reserve requirement you figure out will be based on historical information. The previous year's experience is the most recent, but you will need to adjust it from time to time. Update your reserve needs with a periodic review, perhaps every three months. In January, you'll use the 12-month period from the previous January through December. And in April, you'll set reserve requirements based on the previous April through March. Your reserve should be established as a revolving average, so that the basis for estimates is not too far out of date.

3. Keep Your Perspective on Budgeting

Don't be too critical of yourself if your budget doesn't work out the first time. If you put too little in your reserve, overlook a variable expense, or don't have enough for unexpected bills, you haven't failed, but you do have improved information to use next month. If you learn from the practice of budgeting techniques, you will improve with time. The only failure is not using new information to adjust your procedures.

4. Don't Use Lines of Credit to Pay Expenses

A line of credit may be offered by your local bank or savings and loan and secured by home equity; or offered by a credit card company for your convenience. But unless you use a line of credit wisely, it will make perpetual and growing debt levels all too easy.

Take control of your monthly budget with debt reduction in mind. You may gain a sense of temporary security knowing that extra money is there for you in case you need it. But remember: You can get the same sense of security by setting up your own reserves. If you use budgeting techniques to anticipate expenses as far in advance as possible, you will no longer need to depend on a line of credit or other debt sources.

Lines of credit give you the illusion of month-to-month financial security. But unlike savings and reserves, they represent obligations rather than assets. Being aware of the difference will help you to learn the secret of eliminating debt once and for all, and starting to accumulate net worth. This important principle is the topic of the next chapter.

CHAPTER 5

FOR A RAINY DAY

Money never cometh
out of season.
—*Thomas Draxe*

Here's a situation that just about everyone faces at one time or another: You've been getting through each month one at a time, making payments and trying to add a little money to savings. When you do have a few dollars to put away, something always seems to come up the next month, and you have to use your savings. For example, you lose your job or go out on strike for a month. Then you find yourself saying, "I wish I'd been able to put some money away, so it was there now, when I really need it."

You can begin putting money away for the unexpected interruption of income, for unusual expenses, and for more permanent savings. You can start your plan at once, even if you're in debt. In fact, saving money is an important first step, because it gets you into a savings habit and out of the more destructive spending habit.

Why is it so difficult to save? The main reason is that putting money away becomes a very low priority when income isn't enough to cover today's expenses. We all live with several myths concerning savings. Start by examining these popular myths, and develop a different point of view:

Myth 1: When You're in Debt, Saving Money Is a Very Low Priority
This is misdirected thinking. The debt problem has two sides. First is the lack of a plan for spending money. Second is the

lack of a long-term plan for the accumulation of net worth. Saving money should be one of your highest priorities. It will help you to escape the cycle of debt and to begin managing your money the way you want. When all of your income is spent each month, you're not getting ahead. To make a change, you need to "spend" some of your income on the accumulation of cash assets: savings.

Myth 2: It's Better to Use Any Extra Money to Pay off Debts Rather Than to Save It

The argument here is that you will do better to pay off a credit card on which you're being hit with 18 percent in finance charges than to put money into a 6 percent savings account. The problem, though, is that when you do pay off a debt, you are likely to build it back up again. So instead of building net worth, you're just repeating the same errors, over and over again. No matter how expensive your finance charges are, you need to start a savings plan and keep it going. That's the only way to escape the debt cycle. You will be able to pay off debts *and* save, all within the same monthly budget.

Myth 3: Savings Are for People Who Make More Money Than They Need and Who Can Afford to Put Extra Cash in an Account Every Month

First of all, very few people ever earn more money than they need. As income grows, it's usually accompanied by an increase in the monthly budget, and that action might even outpace the growth in income. Remember, debt problems hit families at all income levels. You're unlikely to ever meet someone who thinks they have extra money to put into savings. Chances are, you will observe that people earning $100,000 per year have debt problems at least as severe as those making $25,000. The problem is still there, but it's on a larger scale.

Myth 4: Savings Are Built up to Improve Your Lifestyle

The belief states that by having savings, it will be possible to pay cash for the things you want but can't afford. Thus, you won't have to go into debt. In fact, savings should be accumulated for two reasons: to create an emergency reserve, either to pay unexpected bills or to see you through periods when income stops; and to build net worth over the long term. Remember the distinction between a solitary sum of money, which is gone once spent, and the personal flexibility to manage money from one month to the next, which is a more permanent advantage. Savings should not be built up with spending in mind. The goal is the accumulation of net worth, ensuring financial freedom.

THE EMERGENCY RESERVE IN YOUR BUDGET

In the last chapter we talked about the budgeting technique of putting aside the same amount each month. Some expenses must be paid quarterly, semi-annually, or annually. The purpose of planning your budget with all expenses in mind is to anticipate variable expenses and to build a reserve for unexpected expenses.

Emergency reserves should be created for another reason: the unexpected loss of income. This can occur in a number of ways. Some examples:

1. You or your spouse are terminated from your job. It may take four to six weeks to find another.
2. You're a union member, and a majority vote to strike. You have no idea how long the strike will last, but it looks like it will be a long one.
3. You are disabled for six months, and the disability policy your employer provides pays only part of your total monthly income.

In any of these events, you will be taken by surprise if you haven't created an emergency reserve fund. It doesn't take long to get into serious budgeting trouble when you don't have income to pay for rent and food, not to mention your other obligations.

Many financial planners and money experts suggest building a reserve equal to three months' income, six months' income, or even what you bring home in a year. These goals are easy to suggest but, as you probably know, very difficult to achieve. And no formula is right for every family.

Your emergency reserve should be matched to your budget and to your obligations. The amount you need to put away will vary with your income, the amount of debt you have to pay off, the time you believe it would take to replace lost income, and your own future goals. Take these steps to figure out how much you need in your emergency reserve:

1. Calculate the level of variable and unexpected expenses you're likely to have in the next 12 months (as explained in the previous chapter). This is the starting point for your emergency reserve fund.

2. Next, set a goal that you will add to your emergency reserve fund to match one week's pay. This amount won't be enough if you're out of work for a month or more, but it's a start.

3. Build your emergency reserve fund to a comfortable level. For example, if you believe you could find another job within two weeks, you will need a fund equal to that pay level. But if you think it could take two months to find another job, your emergency reserve fund should be higher.

4. Review your disability insurance policy. In the event of illness or disability, will you receive enough in benefits to meet your monthly expenses? If not, you should plan to increase insurance protection to an adequate level. This review should be repeated at least once each year. And if you don't have a disability policy, consider looking into it. Premiums are not high and the protection is well worth the price.

SAVINGS IN YOUR BUDGET

To eventually take control of your own finances, you will need to build net worth over time. This process begins with a regular savings plan. Make a clear distinction between your emergency reserve and your savings.

The reserve exists to equalize your monthly expenses, even considering variable and unexpected bills, and to stabilize your budget even if your income is halted temporarily. It's a contingency fund. You should plan to spend it as a way to avoid having to go into debt.

The savings account should be thought of in an opposite way. You want to plan to *not* spend your savings. The account is there to take care of long-term goals, like buying a home, starting your own business, paying for your children's college education, or retiring with financial security and a comfortable lifestyle.

You will want to start putting money aside for emergency and savings purposes as part of today's budget. The problem, of course, is that you have a number of priorities, and you can't meet all of them right now.

1. You want to eliminate existing debts.
2. You want to take charge of your finances and budget so that debt will never get out of hand again.
3. You want to build a cushion into your budget through the creation and maintenance of an emergency reserve fund.
4. You want to start a savings plan.

When we talked about scheduling today's debts for gradual repayment, we brought up the idea of making progress every month—even a little progress. The same idea applies in the creation of reserves and savings. It might be desirable, but not possible, to set up a $2,000 emergency reserve and put $200 per month into savings, just as it's desirable but not possible to pay off all of your debts in the next two weeks.

Build your emergency reserve fund gradually, even when you know the level isn't yet adequate for what you really need. And add *something* to savings every month, even if the amount is lower than what you want to put away. You need to start somewhere. As your debts are gradually brought under control, your ability to save will improve as well.

There are several ways that you can increase the amounts you place in reserves and savings.

1. The Current Budget
Can you afford to put $25 into savings and another $25 into an emergency reserve fund? It will take quite a while to reach

your minimum goal at those levels, but $50 per month is better than nothing. You may have a number of pressing obligations and very little flexibility in today's budget. You will achieve the flexibility you want and need by resolving to save something, even a little, starting this month.

2. Elimination of Debt Payments

By gradually reducing current debts, you will free up ever-growing portions of your income. For example, you may be paying $150 every month to a credit card company. Once the entire debt has been erased, you should be able to save $150 per month—assuming you stop using that card to keep yourself in debt.

3. Income from a Second Job

You might review your budget and conclude that there's simply no way to save anything—at least not until you pay off some of today's debts or earn more money. Considering how critical it is to build a reserve and a savings account, why not take a second job for a few months? Working even one evening per week or half a day on the weekend, you will earn enough to start a modest savings plan.

4. Pay Raises

You've probably noticed that a pay raise doesn't really improve your financial situation. That's because we tend to increase our monthly needs based on the level of income we're earning. When your take-home pay goes up by $50 per month, so do your expenses. But instead of allowing your needs to grow, plan to put the pay raise directly into savings every month and without fail. If you're surviving on today's income level, why not pay yourself when your income goes up?

You can modify the use of extra income so that you accumulate reserves and savings and use part of the money to improve your monthly budget.

Example: One family takes home $1,000 each month and is trying to pay down credit card and department store debts. They're able to put $50 per month into an emergency reserve fund, and another $50 into savings; but that puts quite a strain on their budget. One spouse takes a second job that brings in another $200 per month. Of that total, $100 is used to increase the rate of debt repayments and improve the family's lifestyle moderately. The other $100 is split between emergency reserve and savings, doubling the amounts going to each. When a pay raise of $50 per month is received, the entire amount is put directly into savings:

	Monthly Income	Second Job	Pay Raise	Total
Expenses	$ 900	$100	$ 0	$1,000
Emergency reserve	50	50	0	100
Savings	50	50	50	150
Total	$1,000	$200	$50	$1,250

The combination of a second job and a pay raise represent one-fourth of the original, fixed monthly budget. That's a significant increase in monthly income. With careful planning and control, the family was able to avoid using the extra income unwisely, committing most of it to savings and reserves instead. At the same time, they also put $100 toward their monthly budget, so that the rate of debt repayment would be accelerated. Thus they could afford a few extras now and then.

This plan is illustrated in Figure 5–1. You can devise a similar plan and create an emergency reserve and savings plan without affecting your monthly expense budget.

BUILDING LONG-TERM SAVINGS

We've been discussing very modest amounts of money for savings. It might seem, at first glance, that it's hardly worth the effort to put $100 into savings every month. That's only $1,200 per year. And one medical bill or car repair could wipe that out in a day.

Two points to recognize: First, a savings account should *not*

FIGURE 5–1
The Reserve and Savings Plan

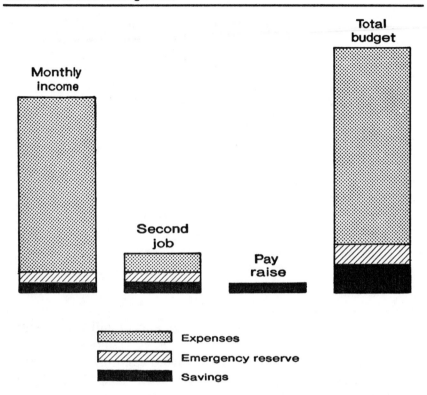

be available, even for unexpected expenses. The money you put away in an emergency reserve is there for those untimely events. But your savings account is a long-term, equity-building plan. Second, saving $100 per month comes out to more than $1,200 per year because you will also be benefiting from the effects of compound interest. And the longer you leave your savings intact, the more rapidly your savings will grow.

The power of compounding can be illustrated with a one-year example. Let's assume your savings account earns 6 percent, and it's compounded every month. That means that at the end of each month, your balance will be increased by 1/2 of 1 percent. You can figure out the monthly interest by dividing 6 percent by 12 months:

$$\frac{6\%}{12} = .50$$

The ½ percent in interest is added to the $100 you deposit at the beginning of the month:

Balance	$100.00
Plus ½%	.50
New balance	$100.50

In the second month, you would add another $100, and interest is then computed on the new balance forward:

Balance	$100.50
Plus deposit	100.00
Total	$200.50
Plus ½%	1.00
New balance	$201.50

When this is carried through for each month, compound interest is calculated on an ever-growing balance. And that balance includes the interest added from each previous month. By the end of the first year, your account will be worth $1,233.56.

The amounts are not large at the beginning, but the overall effect over many years is that your savings will grow at an accelerating rate. After a few years, the monthly interest will be much higher than the amount you're depositing each month. A savings account with a balance of $20,000 will earn $100 per month, if 6 percent interest is compounded monthly. When your account grows beyond that level, interest continues to climb beyond the $100 being saved each month.

A balance of $20,000 might seem like a lot to build at $100 per month. But using the illustration of 6 percent with monthly compounding, it will take less than 12 years to accumulate that much. The total saved after 12 years of deposits at $100 per month is $14,400. But with compound interest, the account's total value will be $21,015, a difference of $6,615 in compound interest.

The rate of compounding is greater when the interest rate is higher than 6 percent. For example, some certificates of deposit, savings bonds, and other savings alternatives may pay 7 or 8 percent, or more.

The table below shows how a $100 deposit made each month will grow over time and at various interest rates. The calculations are based on monthly compounding.

The Effects of Compound Interest

| Year | Amount Saved | Total Value | | |
		6 Percent	7 Percent	8 Percent
5	$ 6,000	$ 6,977	$ 7,159	$ 7,348
10	12,000	16,388	17,308	18,295
15	18,000	29,082	31,696	34,604
20	24,000	46,204	52,093	58,902
25	30,000	69,299	81,007	95,103
30	36,000	100,452	121,997	149,036

To visualize the importance of compound interest for even a modest amount of monthly savings, refer to Figure 5–2. It is based on a monthly deposit of $100, with 6 percent interest compounded monthly. The longer the period, the more rapidly interest compounds. By depositing $36,000 over 30 years, you will build a savings account worth $100,452.

Don't underestimate the importance of starting a savings account today, and never believe that even a small amount is not worth the trouble. If you can afford only $25 per month, or even only $5 or $10, at least you take the first step. As your financial condition improves, you can add to the amounts placed in reserve or in savings.

WHERE TO SAVE

It's probably a good idea to open accounts, both for your emergency reserve and for savings. Keep these funds separate from your checking account, even if you earn interest on that ac-

FIGURE 5–2
Compound Interest

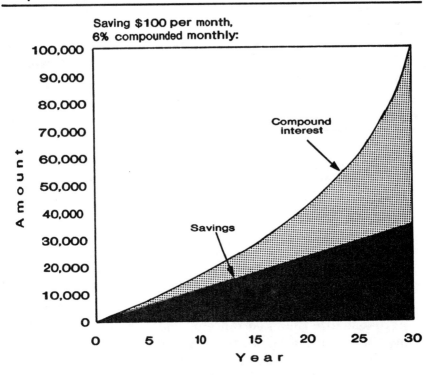

count. Separation is important, because it makes it more difficult for you to break your own rules.

It might also be smart to open different accounts for the reserve and for savings. Remember, the reserve will be spent on equalizing monthly payments, or to replace lost income, but savings should be left intact. If you end up with a reserve that's higher than your anticipated needs in the immediate future, you can always transfer part of the balance to savings. But if the two accounts are put in the same place, you might use part of the savings to pay unexpected current bills. And that's exactly what you want to avoid.

Here are some accounts you can use for emergency reserves and for savings:

1. Passbook Savings Account

This account is easy to open and maintain. You can start an account at a bank, savings and loan association, or credit union, preferably one in which balances are protected by federal insurance. You are guaranteed a set rate of interest, which is usually compounded monthly or quarterly (four times per year). Some accounts compute interest daily, which slightly improves the annual growth of your account's value.

Insurance protection, a guaranteed rate, and the simplicity of savings accounts are major advantages. It's also easy to get your money out, a point worth noting for your emergency reserve fund. Interest you earn in a passbook savings account is taxable each year.

2. Money Market Account or Fund

A money market fund is a form of mutual fund in which many investors deposit funds, and the entire pool is invested in short-term debt instruments issued by corporations or governments. Short term means payment is due within 12 months or less. Many of the investments in a fund's portfolio are turned over in 30 days or less. While these accounts will not be insured, risk is minimal. First, the accounts are managed by professionals who understand the market. Second, the portfolio is well diversified. Third, many of the money market instruments are themselves insured or guaranteed.

Many savings institutions offer money market accounts that work in much the same way as money market mutual funds.

It's easy to get your money out of a money market fund or account. The funds supply you with free checks, and you simply write a check to yourself when you need to make a transfer. There's usually a minimum of either $250 or $500 to make a withdrawal. This type of account is appropriate for an emergency reserve fund and for funds you haven't yet decided how to use or that you will need in the near future.

The dividend paid on your money market fund or account is normally taxed each year as interest. Some funds specialize in tax-free municipal bonds and notes, thus interest is exempt from state and local taxes in many cases.

3. Series EE Bonds

You can purchase EE bonds for as little as $25. The amount you pay represents a discount of the face value of the bond. For example, when you buy an EE bond and pay $25, the maturity value will be $50. And a $100 bond will mature at $200.

You cannot get your money back during the first six months following purchase, except for emergencies. After that, your interest is calculated so that current value goes up each month. The bonds mature in 12 years, and interest rates vary; however, the rate will never fall below $7^{1/2}$ percent.

Series EE bonds are well-suited to building a long-term savings account. They are guaranteed by the full faith and credit of the U.S. government, which makes them one of the safest investments available. Another feature: You have the choice of paying income tax each year on interest earned or deferring income taxes until the bonds mature.

4. Individual Retirement Accounts

Several years ago, you could open an IRA and avoid taxes on the money you invested, up to $2,000 per year. With changes in tax laws, though, not everyone can take advantage of that feature. If your employer contributes to a pension or profit-sharing plan, you are no longer eligible for deductions of amounts invested in IRAs. This may change in the future; but as of 1990, that's the rule.

Even though you might not be able to deduct the amounts you pay in, all earnings are tax-deferred in your IRA. So you can delay income taxes until you remove funds from the IRA account. You can deposit up to $2,000 per year. An IRA will work well for savings accounts, and you have a choice of investments. You can put your IRA money in passbook savings and other forms of interest-bearing accounts; you can buy shares of mutual funds; or you can invest in the stock market through your IRA account. The choice of where to open your IRA should be based on the purpose of the account and the amount of risk you're willing to assume.

5. Certificates of Deposit

Savings institutions offer a variety of time deposit accounts. These pay a higher percentage of interest because you must agree to leave your funds on deposit for a period of time. This may be as short as 30 days or as long as six years or more.

If you withdraw your money early, you will be hit with an interest penalty. Thus, you should plan to use certificates of deposit (CDs) only for savings you are sure you won't need during the contractual term. Interest is taxed in the year earned and paid. CDs can be used to build long-term savings with higher rates than you'll receive in a passbook savings account.

GREEN AND RED RESERVES

We have described money as being green or red. Green money is cash on hand or in savings that you didn't borrow to acquire. And red money is the cash you get by borrowing money.

Emergency reserves and savings can also be either green or red. Remember: Only the green savings really count. For example, you might think you don't need to put aside money for emergencies because you have a line of credit through a credit card or a home equity account. This is not a reserve, but a potential new debt. A line of credit is appropriate in many situations, but only on the assumption that it will be used for temporary debt, which will be repaid very soon. In most cases, unfortunately, lines of credit are misused and lead to problems.

If you draw on your line of credit to pay unexpected or variable bills or to support yourself when you lose your job, you're going further into debt. And that's moving in a direction opposite of where you want to go. You only gain control over your money when you are able to avoid debt. You need to control potential debt, as well as pay off bills you already owe. A line of credit doesn't satisfy that requirement, and it shouldn't be considered as a way to create reserves or savings.

To accumulate real net worth, you need to divide each month's income into three parts. The first you'll use to pay for necessities like food and rent. The second, also part of your budget, is used to reduce the debts you have now. And the third part is used to accumulate net worth through savings and to plan for variations in monthly needs through your emergency reserve.

Constantly be aware of these three parts. Be sure you make some progress each month, by paying off old debts and by putting something into savings and reserves. You also make progress even when you can't afford to reduce debts or save, as long as you don't go any further into debt. That doesn't improve your plan; but when you are able to get from one month to the next without making your debt situation worse, you're on the way to personal financial health.

We've covered savings plans to this point, and shown how different accounts can be used to achieve financial freedom and eliminate dependency on debt. You are probably aware of the problems involved with your checking account as well. It's difficult to stay with a fixed budget when it's so easy to write checks. In the next chapter, you will get some ideas for managing your checking account with your own rules in mind, how to keep your account in balance, and how to use your checking account to create an immediate emergency reserve.

CHAPTER 6

IT'S JUST PAPER

Live within your income,
even if you have to
borrow money to do so.
—*Henry Wheeler Shaw*

Most of your money is never converted to cash. You deposit checks into an account and then write checks against your balance. The total value of bank deposits is far higher than the amount of currency and coin in circulation, so in one sense, most of the money you receive and then pay out *is* just paper.

That doesn't mean noncash money lacks value. The balance in your checking account represents buying power and has tangible value in our economy. But because most of your income and expense transactions flow through your checking account, you need to control your balance carefully. You will want to identify and account for the differences between your checkbook and bank statement every month.

When you don't know how much money you have in your checking account, you are not in control. In this chapter, we'll remove the mystery from the process of reconciliation (balancing), and show you how to gain and keep control over your paper money.

BUILDING A STARTING BALANCE

The first step in gaining control is to establish an accurate beginning balance. If you don't have this, you will never be able to identify the amount you have at the end of the following month. There is no point in even attempting to reconcile this month's bank statement if you haven't identified and corrected older problems.

If you have not balanced your account in several months, you need to establish a "good" balance first. One of the reasons for reconciling is to ensure that both your errors and the bank's errors are accounted for and corrected. Even with automation, banks can still make mistakes, and they sometimes do. But if you haven't been taking care of your account every month, you will have to start out by giving the bank the benefit of the doubt.

Establishing a balance forward is quite simple. Even the most ignored account can be brought under control with these steps:

1. Gather Your Bank Statements for the Last Six Months

The statement you receive each month reports all of the deposits, checks, and adjustments entered by the bank. Your bank either sends checks back to you, or lists the checks that have cleared. In either case, you can account for all of the checks that have been cashed in the six-month period.

If you have not kept your statements for six months, you can get copies from your bank. You do not need the actual cleared checks, only the statements.

2. Make a List of All Uncleared Checks

Since most banks list checks in numerical order, this task is an easy one. Some checks written in one month won't clear until the next, so part of your reconciliation requires isolating and listing uncleared checks as of the end of the six months.

Don't count any checks you wrote before the six-month period. They probably cleared the bank before the period, and should not be considered as still outstanding. Most of the checks on your list will have been written in the last month, and a few might still be uncleared from two months ago.

3. Compare Deposits for the Last Two Months

Banks record deposits as they are received. If you make a deposit on the cut-off date (the date the bank prepares your statement), that deposit might show up in the following month.

Make sure that all of your deposits are listed on the bank statement. If you made a deposit at the end of the latest month and it doesn't show up, it's in transit and will be listed as the first deposit on next month's statement.

4. Figure out Your Balance Forward

Write down the ending balance shown on your latest bank statement. Then add any deposits in transit (amounts you deposited that are not shown on the statement).

Next, subtract the total of checks that have not cleared the bank. If a check is very old, it probably cleared several months ago and should not be included here.

Add deposits in transit to the bank's ending balance. Then subtract outstanding checks. This is your constructed balance forward, your starting point.

Use the worksheet shown in Figure 6–1 to construct a balance forward in your checking account.

CHECKBOOK MAINTENANCE

Now that you have a good starting point, you will be able to account for all of the differences between your balance and the balance the bank says you have—every month and without fail. Balancing the two sides requires some work, for several reasons:

1. It isn't always easy to understand how an adjustment affects your balance.
2. Finding addition or subtraction errors takes time and effort; you might go over a list of checks several times before you find the problem.
3. If there are several deposits in transit or outstanding checks, the job is harder than when you only have a few items to balance.

FIGURE 6–1
Worksheet: Balance Forward

Worksheet: Balance Forward

Balance, latest bank statement $_____

Plus: deposits in transit   +_____

Less: outstanding checks

_____   _____
_____   _____
_____   _____
_____   _____
_____   _____
_____   _____
_____   _____
_____

          total   −_____

Balance forward $_____

The better you manage your bank account, the easier it will be to keep it under control. Here are a few tips to help make the job easier.

1. Know Your Bank's Cut-Off Date
Plan to write monthly checks according to when your bank prepares your statement. This will reduce the number of outstanding checks each month. For example, if your bank's cut-off date is the 26th, don't write 15 checks on the 24th. They will probably all end up as timing differences. Wait until the 27th to reduce the number of checks you'll have to include on your list. Your goal should be to reduce the number of items you'll have to adjust.

2. Always Start with a Good Balance
You can balance your account only if last month's problems have been identified and solved. For example, if your bank charged you $16.00 last month for printing a new supply of checks, that adjustment has to be made to your balance. You need to identify it, and then reduce your balance by $16.00. If you don't take that step, you'll be off by the same amount again this month because the balance in your checkbook will be wrong.

3. Check and Double-Check Your Math
Besides the timing differences between your records and the bank's, the most common reconciling problem comes from math errors. Check your math throughout the month before trying to balance your account.

Look for the common errors: adding checks instead of subtracting them; transposing numbers (writing down 723 instead of 732, for example); writing down the wrong amount; and simple addition or subtraction errors. Use a calculator if necessary to double-check your math.

4. Check the Math in Your Reconciliation
Besides ensuring correct math in your checkbook, also check your addition and subtraction on the reconciliation itself. You won't balance if you make a math or transposition error on a list of outstanding checks, or if you have a math error on your summary.

MASTERING TIMING DIFFERENCES

Balancing your account may be frustrating mainly because you're not sure how to treat timing differences or adjustments. But once you master the significance of a transaction, you will overcome this problem.

Timing differences come about from two events: the deposit in transit and the outstanding check. By identifying the month-to-month recording of deposits and checks, you will be able to reconcile between the bank and your own records.

Example: You deposit your paycheck every two weeks. In May and June, you made the following deposits:

Date	Amount
5–3	$598
5–17	611
5–31	618
6–15	623
6–29	605

The bank statements you received in May and June do not agree with your totals. They show the following deposits:

May	June
$598	$618
611	623

Because the bank's cut-off date is at the end of the month, your deposits do not always show up in the same month they were made. Remember, the bank will record deposits (and checks) only when they know about the transaction. If a deposit is made on the cut-off date, it may not be recorded until the following day. Comparing your record to the bank's shows how this timing difference works:

	Your Record	Bank Record	Timing Difference
May			
	$598	$598	
	611	611	
	618	—	+$618
June			
	—	$618	−$618
	$623	623	
	605	—	+$605

The last deposit for $605 will show up on the July bank statement. Notice how a timing difference comes up at the end of May and cancels out in June. At the time you balance your bank account, you need to allow for this by adding the deposit in transit to the balance reported by the bank.

The same type of adjustment works with outstanding checks, although the adjustment is a reduction of the bank's reported balance rather than an increase.

Example: Last month, you wrote several checks during the week before the bank's cut-off date. These did not show up on the bank statement and, accordingly, will not be included in the list of checks the bank recorded. They will be posted in the month they clear the bank. Your outstanding checks are:

Check	Amount
507	$ 34.15
508	101.00
509	77.11
511	8.89
512	20.00
Total	$241.15

To reconcile for this timing difference, you need to reduce the balance reported by the bank. Those checks were written, but they haven't come through the banking system yet. When they do come through, the bank will reduce your balance.

Assuming that the bank reported an ending balance of $415.62, the deposit and check-timing differences would be reconciled in this way:

Ending balance (bank)	$415.62
Plus deposit in transit	+605.00
Less outstanding checks	−241.15
Corrected ending balance	$779.47

This should be the correct balance, assuming the bank did not make any errors. If your checking account balance does not agree with this balance, you need to make adjustments for errors and charges.

MASTERING ADJUSTMENTS

Timing differences are only part of the reconciliation process. You also need to account for and correct any adjustments. These may arise because the bank adjusted your balance for returned checks, printed check fees, or service charges. Or you might find adjustments due to math errors in your checkbook.

You should adjust according to the way the bank makes their adjustment entry. A *debit* on your bank statement (also called a charge) is a reduction in the account. To correct your balance, deduct a debit adjustment. Typical debits include monthly service fees and returned checks. A *credit* adjustment is an addition to your balance. To record it in your checkbook, add a credit amount. For example, if your bank pays interest on checking account balances, you will need to add the amount reported each month on your bank statement.

Remember, reconciling for adjustments is a two-step process. First, the adjustment must be found and identified as either a debit (reduction in your balance) or credit (increase in your balance). Second, the adjustment must be entered in your checkbook, or you won't be able to balance your account next month.

You may discover an error made by the bank. For example, someone else's check might be charged against your account, or a deposit may be recorded for the wrong amount or left off the statement altogether. In these cases, you need to contact the bank, point out the error, and ask for a correcting adjustment. You do not need to correct your checkbook balance in the event of a bank error, but you do need to ensure that the correction is made so that you will be able to balance the account next month.

THE RECONCILIATION FORM

The easiest way to reconcile your bank account is to enter plus and minus charges to the bank's balance for all timing differences, and then to adjust your checkbook balance for all adjustments. If this is done correctly, both sides will show the same total.

A sample of the bank reconciliation form is shown in Figure 6–2. Notice that there are two parts: the bank's and your checkbook.

The first line, "Balance on bank statement," is the ending balance reported by your bank. Add to this the total of unrecorded deposits (usually those made at the end of the month)

FIGURE 6–2
Bank Reconciliation

Bank Reconciliation

Balance on bank statement	$_____
Plus: unrecorded deposits	+_____
Less: outstanding checks	–_____
Balance	$_____
Balance in checkbook	$_____
Plus: Interest	+_____
Less: service charge	–_____
Less: check printing fee	–_____
Math errors	+(–)_____
Less: returned checks	–_____
Other _____	_____
_____	_____
Balance	$_____

and subtract the total of outstanding checks (all checks you have written that have not yet cleared the bank).

To prepare an accurate list of outstanding checks, follow these steps:

1. Find the list of checks cleared this month on your bank statement. Most banks provide this information in numerical order.
2. Identify those checks listed as outstanding last month. Place a check mark next to the amounts, making sure they agree with the amounts you listed on last month's bank reconciliation.
3. Refer to your checkbook. Place a check mark on the bank statement for each check you wrote that also appears on the statement. Also place a check mark by each amount in the checkbook. Make sure the amount of each cleared check agrees with the amount you recorded in your checkbook.
4. Prepare your new list of outstanding checks. It should include all the checks written during the month that did not appear on the bank statement.

The second section is a reconciliation of your checkbook balance. The adjustments listed are the most common types of adjusting entries you need to make. When you have correctly added credit adjustments and subtracted debit adjustments, your checkbook balance should agree with the corrected bank balance.

The balancing process is logical. You just have to account for all entries on both sides—your checkbook and the bank. In between, you will have timing differences and adjustments. But in some cases, you will check and double-check, and your account just won't balance. You then need to follow a few steps to isolate the problem.

WHEN THE BALANCES DON'T AGREE

Even when following the procedure for proper bank reconciliation, you won't always be successful the first time. When you aren't, use this checklist:

1. Check your balances forward. Are you starting with a good balance, one in which your checkbook and the bank statement were, in fact, reconciled?
2. Have you entered adjustments in your checkbook? Were they made in the right direction or did you reverse one or more by mistake?
3. Check the amounts of all deposits and checks between the bank statement and your checkbook. They should all be in agreement, including those checks listed on last month's and this month's outstanding checks list.
4. Check all of your math—again. Review math in your checkbook *and* on your reconciliation forms.
5. Check this month's adjustments. Did you enter all of them on the reconciliation form? Did you add credits and subtract debits?
6. Did you void or stop payment on any checks this month? If so, make sure they're not on your list of outstanding checks. Also make sure you added the check amount to your balance.
7. Were any of your deposits returned? If so, you need to subtract the amount from your checkbook. If you re-deposited a bounced check, be sure it was entered again. Also be sure it wasn't entered twice by mistake.

Another step that will help find unreconciled items is to isolate the plus and minus transactions, both on the bank statement and in your checkbook. Then check both sides to find out where you're still out of balance. Your bank will include a summary on the statement showing the balance forward, additions (deposits and credits), subtractions (checks and debits), and the new balance. Compare this to the plus and minus entries in your checkbook.

Use a balancing worksheet like the one shown in Figure 6–3 to find out where adjustments need to be made. The bank's entries are shown in the two left columns, and your checkbook entries should be written in on the two right columns.

Add up the total of deposits and the total of checks in your checkbook to find the totals you need for this form. When you have completed it, check the accuracy of your math with these steps:

FIGURE 6–3
Balancing Worksheet

Balancing Worksheet

| | BANK STATEMENT | | CHECKBOOK | |
	Deposits	Checks	Deposits	Checks
Total this month				
Timing differences:				
unrecorded deposits:				
this month	+		+	
last month	−			
outstanding checks:				
this month		+		
last month		−		
Adjustments:				
interest credited			+	
returned checks			−	
service charges				+
check printing fee				+
math errors				
other adjustments:				
Reconciled balance				

1. Write down the balance forward in your checkbook as of the beginning of the month (this balance should be the point at which you balanced the account last month).
2. Add the total of all deposits you listed and other credits you added in the checkbook.
3. Subtract the total of all checks you wrote and other debits you subtracted from your balance.
4. The remainder should agree with the ending balance in your checkbook. If it does not, there's an error, either in the checkbook math, or in the steps you just took. Find the error and correct it.

The checkbook side is summarized in these steps:

1. Beginning balance   _____
2. Plus deposits and credits   + _____
3. Less checks and debits   − _____
4. Ending balance   _____

To isolate the error, begin by writing in the timing differences—unrecorded deposits and outstanding checks. Note that we have included a space for deposits on the checkbook side in case you forgot to add in a deposit you made during the month in your checkbook.

In this format, you also need to balance timing differences between the two months. Thus, both deposit and check-timing differences on the bank side require adding this month's totals *and* deducting last month's timing difference totals. When this is done, the bank totals should agree with your checkbook totals on both sides.

The second part of the worksheet involves adjustments. Enter all of the debits shown on the bank statement as additional payments to the checkbook side; and enter all credits on the bank statement as additional credits to the checkbook side. There is also space for "other" adjustments, which may include corrections of errors in the checkbook as well as those made by the bank.

Using this procedure, you will be able to determine whether an undiscovered error will be found in the plus side (deposits and other credits) or in the minus side (checks and other debits).

Another worksheet you might find useful is the daily balance record. This is a summary of each day's deposits, checks, and adjustments. A sample of this form is shown in Figure 6–4.

Complete this form each month. Every day on which you make a deposit, write a check, or otherwise adjust your balance, write an explanation and enter the amount. Explanations should include a range of checks written, identification of a deposit, or the nature of an adjustment. Carry your balance forward throughout the month, adjusting the balance by adding everything entered in the plus column, and subtracting everything entered in the minus column. Before trying to balance your bank account, add the totals of each column and make

FIGURE 6–4
Daily Balance Record

Daily Balance Record

Month _____

DATE	EXPLANATION	+		BALANCE
Total				

sure your ending balance is correct. The starting balance forward, plus the total of the " + " column, less the total of the " − " column, should equal your ending balance.

The daily balance record will help you complete the balancing worksheet at the end of the month. The daily record is also worth the effort in these circumstances:

- You have a lot of problems with math and need a procedure to keep yourself in balance from one day to the next.
- The type of checkbook you use does not include space to keep a running balance.
- You find it easier to complete a reconciliation when all of your checkbook entries are shown on a single page.

The daily balance record will just be extra work if none of these situations apply to you, or if it duplicates the records you're already keeping in your checkbook.

PROPER USE OF YOUR ACCOUNT

Having a checking account is virtually a necessity today. It's inconvenient to get through a month without having checks, and it's not wise to keep a large amount of cash around the house. Properly used and controlled, your checking account is a convenience. But if misused, it can keep you in debt and prevent you from taking control over your finances.

Your checking account should be a conduit for the paper money you receive and pay out each month. Your budget should determine your goal for each expense category, not the balance available in your account. Here are some suggestions for maintaining control over your checking account, and for staying within the budget you have developed for yourself.

1. Don't Take the Checkbook to the Store if You Have the Cash to Buy What You Need

A good budgeting technique is to know in advance of a shopping trip about how much you will need. Go to the bank beforehand and cash a check for the amount you have budgeted; then pay the bill in cash. This works well for weekly food shopping, where overspending from your checkbook may be a chronic problem.

2. Don't Use Your Account Like a Line of Credit, Even When You Have Overdraft Protection

Overdraft protection may be a very practical convenience, especially if you run into a cash flow problem in the week immediately before you're paid. But you should also plan to pay back any advances in the week after taking them. If you do not exercise control, your overdraft "protection" will end up as another source of escalating and recurring debt. Don't think of using this feature except in a rare emergency.

3. Don't Overdraw Your Account, and Don't Depend on the "Float" to Get through the Month

You should never overdraw your checking account, even if you believe that some checks haven't yet cleared. You have no control over the time required for checks to get back to your bank, and using the "float" (the balance of outstanding checks) to get from one paycheck to the next is a dangerous habit.

4. Be Sure You Know How the Banking System Works and What Your Balance Represents

Your bank balance is the net of deposits you make, less checks you write, adjusted for service charges, returned checks, interest credited, and other debits and credits. While this might seem obvious to most people, there are some who don't understand this concept. Remember, there is really no mystery to the way that your checking account works.

A case history that illustrates this point: One young couple were advised by the bank that their account was several hundred dollars overdrawn. "That's impossible," they replied. "We have a balance of more than $200 in the account."

When they visited the bank to straighten out the problem, the account representative questioned several deposits written in the checkbook that did not appear on the bank statement. The answer: "We ran out of money, so we increased the balance." They simply wrote down the amount needed to stay in the black but didn't deposit money in the bank.

5. Open an Account That Does Not Charge Monthly Fees but Does Pay Interest on Your Balance

With the competition for accounts in today's banking and savings industry, you should be able to find an institution that will not charge a monthly fee but that will pay interest on your balance. Most will require a minimum deposit, usually $500 or more. If your daily balance is lower than the minimum, you will not be paid interest at all—no matter how high your balance was on other days. And the minimum balance may also be a requirement to avoid service charges on the account.

6. Build a Cushion into Your Account

We've discussed emergency reserve funds as a smart idea for evening out your expense budget, even when expense levels vary from one month to another. A second way to allow for unexpected or variable expenses is to build a cushion into your account balance.

You can do this gradually. This month, add $50 into your account, but don't record it as part of the balance. Next month, add another $50. Continue this until you have built up the reserve you want.

This idea should be put into practice only when you have an interest-bearing account; otherwise, you're not putting your money to work for you. As long as you keep track of the amount of cushion, you won't have a problem balancing your bank account. At the end of the month, your recorded balance should be lower than the right balance by the amount of the reserve.

A properly used checking account that's balanced at the end of the month gives you control and convenience. But it's easy to misuse the account. Managing paper money is not difficult. It requires setting standards for yourself and then living by them.

Another problem you may face, even while trying to get out of debt and stay there, is the way you use plastic money— credit cards, debit cards, and revolving accounts. The next chapter offers guidelines for management and control of plastic money.

CHAPTER 7

PLASTIC SURGERY

Never buy anything
you can't lift.
—*John Bear*

It's easy to get credit. That's one of the reasons that so many people have chronic debt problems. When credit card companies make it easy for you to get into debt, they also make it easier for you to stay there.

The solution is to understand how credit cards work and how they should be used. You may have to change your charging habits or, in some cases, cancel your accounts and throw your cards away. Having a credit card is a convenience and you can use it wisely—as long as you are able to stay out of debt at the same time.

In this chapter you will see how expensive it is to pay only the minimum required balance on your card. We will explain how to protect your account against fraud and theft. And we will provide guidelines for management of revolving credit.

The availability of credit has a direct consequence in the amount of mony you are able to save or invest. According to the U.S. Department of Commerce, the average family saved 7 percent of its discretionary income during the 1970s. But by the end of the 1980s, we saved only 4 percent. (Discretionary income is the amount left over after paying income taxes, also called "disposable" income.)

Why are we saving less now than 10 years ago? One answer may be the substantial increase in debts we owe. The Federal Reserve Board reports that total debts in the public sector, including home mortgages, credit and store charge accounts, and personal loans, grew from $1.4 trillion dollars at the beginning of the 1980s, to $3.2 trillion near the end of the decade. At the end of 1981, public debt was about 58 percent of total personal income. Now, it's more than 90 percent.[1]

You can escape the trend toward increasing debt and decreasing savings by establishing your own rules and standards for using credit, and staying with your plan.

Following your plan will not only cut down on your interest expenses and overall debt, it will also help you to avoid repeating past mistakes in the future.

CREDIT CARD COMPANIES

The first step is to recognize the business that credit card companies are in. They are lenders. They earn a profit from the finance charges you pay every month, and as long as you keep your accounts current, they don't mind the fact that you get into debt and stay there.

Even large department store chains that sell through revolving accounts are in the lending business. A large portion of profits are derived not from the markups on merchandise, but from interest.

The convenience of charging a purchase might seem like a valuable advantage. It allows you to buy merchandise that you couldn't otherwise afford to pay for this month, and it helps you to keep your money for necessities like food and rent. At least, that's the argument that we hear in ads promoting credit. We are encouraged to go into debt and to stay there.

For example, if you have a credit card, you already know how a maximum is increased. If you have paid the minimum required amount each month, you can ask for a higher credit limit, and it will probably be granted. Some companies automatically give you a higher limit when your balance reaches

---

[1]Source: *Finance Facts Yearbook* published by American Financial Services Association, quoting statistics from the U.S. Department of Commerce and from the Federal Reserve Board.

the previous limit. And if you pay off the entire amount, the credit card company might just raise your limit again.

All of this is designed to make it easy for you to go into debt, to use the company's money at a price. The credit card companies and stores that offer revolving credit accounts would not make any profit from finance charges if you didn't allow a balance to go forward to the next month.

Lenders—including credit card companies—encourage you to think of debt as convenience by offering attractive features, like free or low-cost insurance, credits for every dollar you charge, and even free mileage credit through airlines offering frequent flyer programs. These lenders also have come up with innovations to attract more customers. Besides the revolving credit account, you can get a straight line of credit through the banks and other companies offering accounts. They supply you with free checks, which you can write for any reason. Then you receive a monthly statement with interest charged from the date you used funds. You are required to repay a minimum balance each month.

Another twist is the debit card. Unlike the credit account, with which you are borrowing money and then paying interest, the debit card is a form of automatic draft. Each time you use the debit card, funds are removed from your checking or savings account. The balance in your account is a form of "debit limit" (similar to the credit limit on the credit card). Some companies combine credit and debit features, allowing you to spend more than you have in checking or savings.

AVOIDING CREDIT CARD FRAUD

Using your credit (or debit) card wisely requires taking a few precautions. Fraud and theft are widespread, and it's very easy for someone to get your number, duplicate a card, and then use it to buy merchandise or get cash advances. A good general rule is to protect credit cards with the same degree of care you use to protect your cash.

One scam is run by telephone. You receive a call from someone claiming to be an employee of the credit card company. You are offered low-cost protection in the event your card is lost or stolen. The caller asks for your card number. A variation: Someone calls and says you have won a free gift or vacation. But to reserve your prize, they need your credit card number.

A smart rule to follow is: Never give out your card number to someone who telephones you. If you order merchandise by phone and make a call yourself, you can charge your purchase. But be very cautious when you receive a call. The person on the other end can easily duplicate your credit card using your number, and then use it to make purchases.

Also be careful when you use your card in a store. Watch the transaction and make sure the clerk doesn't run your card through the machine twice. Also be sure that the card returned to you is your card.

Keep all of your receipts and compare them to your monthly bill. If you cannot identify a transaction, write a letter to the credit card company and ask them to investigate the charge. (Your request must be in writing to protect your rights.) Watch out for duplicate charges on your account.

One individual stole hundreds of dollars while working as a clerk and earning minimum wage. When a customer paid for merchandise with a credit card, he ran off two slips. One was put aside. At the end of the day, the clerk forged the customer's signature on the second slip. He knew that most people would catch the error if the extra charge went through in the same month, so he waited four weeks and then filled out the slip, for exactly the same amount as the original purchase. Even those people who would remember making the purchase would often not question the charge. The amount agreed. On the day the clerk placed the forged slip into the cash register, he removed that amount of cash. Thus, the register balanced for the day, and the theft was difficult to catch—unless the customer did match slips to charges and found the duplication.

This form of fraud might be more common than anyone knows because most people do not keep their slips and check their statement carefully. If you do not take the precaution of checking everything carefully, you may be putting money into the thief's hands, and it will never be detected.

If the store uses carbon copies for your duplicate, ask for the carbon, and then destroy it. Don't trust anyone else to destroy the carbon for you. Thieves often go through garbage cans behind stores, looking for carbon copies from which to create duplicate cards.

In the event that your credit card is stolen, you must notify the issuing company within two days. If you do this, you cannot be charged more than $50, no matter how high the balance goes. You should keep a list of all your credit card numbers, issuer names, and toll-free telephone numbers. Keep this list somewhere safe so that you can immediately notify companies if your cards are lost or stolen.

You probably do not need to buy protection plans offered by many companies. All they will do in the event your cards are lost is contact the issuer in the same way that you would do. If you write down the card numbers and make the call, you do not need additional protection.

Every company that issues credit cards provides a telephone number on the back of its monthly statement, along with complete instructions for reporting lost or stolen cards. Fill out a credit card record like the one shown in Figure 7–1, and keep it somewhere safe.

If your card is issued by one of the national companies, call the toll-free number listed below:

American Express	1-800-528-2121
Diners Club and	1-800-525-9150
Carte Blanche	1-800-332-9340 (Colorado)
Discover	1-800-858-5588
MasterCard	1-800-826-2181
Visa	1-800-336-8472 (Classic)
	1-800-847-2911 (Gold)

Some additional precautions:

- When you cancel your account, notify the company to avoid annual charges. Cut the card in half so that no one else can use it.
- Don't lend your card to someone else or allow them to use your account number.

FIGURE 7–1
Credit Card Record

Credit Card Record			
COMPANY	**CARD NUMBER**	**EXPIRATION DATE**	**PHONE**

- Don't leave your card where someone else might find it. Keep current cards in your wallet or purse.
- Cancel accounts for cards you do not need.

It's not wise to carry a large amount of cash with you, nor do you need to keep a number of active accounts. If you have more than two credit card accounts, consider cancelling the ones that charge the highest annual fees and monthly interest.

USING CREDIT CARDS WISELY

Your credit card should be thought of as the availability of revolving debt. If you misuse the credit given to you, debts can be paid off but they are likely to come back in a few months. In fact, you may remain in debt because of the perpetual nature of this form of credit.

Example: Last year, you asked for a personal loan to consolidate your credit card debts. Today, you are still making monthly payments on your bank loan, but your credit card balances are back at the maximum again.

Example: You planned to pay $100 per month until your credit card balance was paid down to zero, but you also continued to use the card, and today the minimum payment is up to $135. Not only has the plan not worked; you owe more money now than when you started your plan.

Follow these guidelines for wise control of your credit cards:

1. Remember That Using the Card Is One of the Ways You Go into Debt
Many people describe their debt problems as something that sneaked up on them. They owe a lot of money, but they don't even know where it was spent. That's because credit cards are *too* easy to use. Only by recognizing that every charge puts you further into debt will you be able to escape this cycle.

2. Remember Your Budget
Your monthly budget sets restrictions on what you will allow yourself to spend each month. But a credit card can destroy your budget if you use it too often and for the wrong purchases. Use your credit card only to the extent that you have allowed for in your budget. Avoid any purchase outside of that limitation.

3. Think of Your Card as a Back-Up Reserve
You may think of your credit card as a back-up emergency source of borrowed money. For example, your car breaks down and you have to spend $500 for repairs. You need your car for work, and you don't have the money in your emergency reserve fund. In this case, use your card. Then revise your budget and come up with a repayment schedule you can afford. But also avoid using the same card for other purchases until the balance has been repaid.

4. Pay in Cash or by Check When You Can

A lot of people pull out their credit card automatically whenever they go to the store. Then, when the monthly statement arrives, they discover that they owe several hundred dollars. That's how your spending habits go out of control and ruin your monthly budget. Use credit cards only for specific emergencies or budgeted purchases. For anything else, pay in cash or by check.

5. Don't Buy What You Don't Need

You may be aware of poor buying habits in the past, and you might even make a resolution to stop buying impulsively. But then you see a sale that's too good to pass up, and out comes the credit card. Think of your card as a form of cash—cash going *out* of your pocket—because when your monthly statement arrives, that's exactly what it will become. Don't buy what you don't need, and try not to exceed your monthly budget.

6. Set Your Own Credit Limit

Forget about that $4,000 limit you have on your credit card. Based on the limitations of your budget, set a limit for yourself. If you cannot afford to spend more than $200 per month through your credit card, cut yourself off when you reach that level. This will give you a degree of control that most credit card holders never achieve.

7. Use the Reserve Method for Repayment

You already understand how to set up a reserve for emergency expenses and also to equalize your monthly budget, even when some expenses hit quarterly or once per year. You can use the reserve method to equalize credit card repayments as well.

Example: You have budgeted for an average monthly expense of $200 on your credit card. Based on last year's spending pattern, you expect to charge most items between January and April. Set aside $200 per month for repayment of your credit card debt.

Here is one way this could work out for the coming year:

Credit Card Reserve

Month	Amount Charged	Less: Payment	Plus: 19.5% Interest	Balance
January	$ 265	$ 200	$ 0	$ 65
February	218	200	1	84
March	495	200	1	380
April	709	200	6	895
May	0	200	15	710
June	105	200	12	627
July	92	200	10	529
August	0	200	9	338
September	0	200	5	143
October	0	145*	2	0
November	0	0*	0	0
December	0	0*	0	0
Total	$1,884	$1,945	$61	

*When a payment of less than $200 is required, the difference is deposited in the emergency reserve account.

In this example the emergency reserve at the end of the year will contain $255—the difference between the $200 per month committed to paying the card balance, and the amount actually paid throughout the year.

SCHEDULING REPAYMENTS

Any lender offering a revolving credit account will also offer a convenient repayment schedule. This convenience is very expensive. Interest rates may run as high as 18 to 20 percent, and the minimum monthly payment is computed as a percentage of the total balance. Thus, as your balance is paid down, the minimum payment also falls. Your repayment term will be stretched out over many months or years. Interest is computed on the outstanding balance at the beginning of the month.

In comparison, when a loan is arranged with an equal monthly payment, the balance will be paid off more quickly. Again, the monthly interest is computed on the monthly balance; but over time, more of the total payment goes toward the balance, and less goes to interest.

Even a home mortgage works in this way. The payments you make during the first few years are mostly for interest, and only a small amount goes toward principal. In fact, in a 30-year mortgage with 10 percent interest, you have paid only one-half of the total debt after 25 years.

The problem with reducing the monthly payment on credit card debts has several sides:

1. It takes longer to pay off the entire debt because the rate of repayment slows down as your balance falls.

2. You may use the card while making the minimum payment, so that any progress in eliminating the debt is replaced by more debt. You end up at the maximum, committed to making monthly payments for money you spent several months ago.

3. The lenders will not be concerned with a repayment schedule that lasts many years because they are earning a very decent return on their money. They are only concerned with one thing: that you make the minimum payment each month.

4. The minimum payment plan does not help you to control your money within your budget. You are better off freezing use of your card and paying more than the minimum in the same amount each month. This will make a substantial difference in the total amount of interest you will pay.

To show how interest expense defeats your plan to get out of debt, you will need to understand how that interest is computed each month. Your credit card comany tells you the annual rate; but you pay interest on outstanding balances each month. Thus, the annual rate is divided by 12 (months), and that monthly rate is applied to your balance. The interest is added, and any payments you make are subtracted.

Example: Your credit card company charges an annual rate of 19.5 percent. Your balance this month is $4,500, and you have decided to stop using the card until the balance has been paid off. You are required to pay a minimum balance each month equal to no less than 3 percent of the outstanding balance, or $20, whichever is less.

The monthly rate is computed by dividing the annual rate by 12 (months). To perform the math, first figure out the decimal equivalent of the annual rate. To do this, move the decimal point two places to the left:

$$19.5\% = .195 \text{ (decimal equivalent)}$$

Now divide by 12:

$$\frac{.195}{12} = .01625$$

This is the monthly rate that is applied to your outstanding balance. Your finance charge is 1.625 percent of the debt.

How long will it take you to repay this debt if you make the minimum required payment? You might be surprised to learn that it will take 15 years and seven months to reduce the balance to zero. During the first year, you will reduce your balance by $690, but your total payments will be $1,503. The debt will be amortized very slowly. (Amortization is the term used to describe the scheduled repayment of a debt.) The first year's payments will be:

Amortization Schedule

Month	Plus: 19.5% Interest	Less: 3% Payment	Balance
Balance			$4,500
January	$ 73	$ 134	4,439
February	72	133	4,378
March	71	131	4,318
April	70	130	4,258
May	69	128	4,199
June	68	126	4,141
July	67	124	4,084
August	66	123	4,027
September	65	121	3,971
October	65	119	3,917
November	64	118	3,863
December	63	116	3,810
Total	$813	$1,503	

Each month's interest increases the balance, and each month's payment reduces it. That's why the payments totaling $1,503 only reduced the debt by $690. More was paid in interest than in reducing the debt.

The figures in the table were computed in the following manner:

Monthly payment =
    Balance forward × .03 (3%, the minimum
                required payment)

Monthly interest =
Previous balance × .06125 (the annual
rate, 19.5 percent,
divided by 12
months)

Balance forward =
Previous balance
+ Interest for the month
− Payment made during the month

Over a total of 15 years and seven months, you would pay
the amount shown in the following table:

Schedule for Full Repayment (minimum payment per month)

Year	Interest	Payments	Balance
Forward			$4,500
1	$ 813	$1,503	3,810
2	689	1,273	3,226
3	584	1,077	2,733
4	494	911	2,316
5	420	775	1,961
6	355	655	1,661
7	302	555	1,408
8	255	470	1,193
9	216	398	1,011
10	183	337	857
11	155	286	726
12	131	246	611
13	108	240	479
14	80	240	319
15	45	240	124
16	8	132	0
Total	$4,838	$9,338	

Annual payments in the last few years even out because
the minimum of $20 per month is made when 3 percent of the
outstanding balance is at or below that level.

What will the difference be if you decide to pay $200 per
month until the loan is repaid? Several changes will take place:

1. Total repayment will require two years and five months,
   or more than 13 years less than under the minimum
   payment plan.

2. Total of payments will be $5,647, or about $3,700 less than the minimum payment plan.
3. The difference in total payments is interest, which will be only $1,147 instead of $4,838.

The more rapidly you amortize a debt, the less you pay in interest and the more quickly that debt will be erased. Each month's interest is based on the amount of balance unpaid. So it makes a lot of sense to control not only the amount of debt you incur, but the method of getting rid of previous debts. When you accelerate repayment, you will cut months, perhaps many years off the time you will remain in debt. And you also reduce your overall interest rate.

Some people argue that it's better to continue making the minimum payment and taking an income tax deduction. But remember, you will spend less by reducing interest, and consumer interest is not fully deductible.

The table below shows how much more rapidly your balance will be paid down at the rate of $200 per month, just during the first year:

Amortization Schedule

Month	Plus: 19.5% Interest	Less: $200 Payment	Balance
Balance			$4,500
January	$ 73	$ 200	4,373
February	71	200	4,244
March	69	200	4,113
April	67	200	3,980
May	65	200	3,845
June	62	200	3,707
July	60	200	3,567
August	58	200	3,425
September	56	200	3,281
October	53	200	3,134
November	51	200	2,985
December	49	200	2,834
Total	$734	$2,400	

On this schedule, the debt will fall more rapidly. The entire debt will be repaid in two years and five months:

Schedule for Full Repayment ($200 payment each month)

Year	Interest	Payments	Balance
Forward			$4,500
1	$ 734	$2,400	2,834
2	378	2,400	812
3	35	847	0
Total	$1,147	$5,647	

COMPUTING AMORTIZATION

To compute the rate of amortization on your own credit cards, you can apply the same technique we have used to illustrate our example. This is a useful exercise, not only to figure out what you are paying on your credit card debt, but also to plan for a more rapid, budgeted repayment schedule. The exercise will give you a fair estimate of your interest expense. In practice, however, your credit card company probably computes interest from the day you charged each purchase. Thus, your estimate may not agree with the amount actually charged.

The formula for loan amortization may look intimidating at first glance. But if you break it down into the steps involved, it is not difficult. The steps are:

1. Figure out the monthly interest. Divide the annual rate by 12.
2. Multiply the previous balance by the monthly rate to arrive at this month's interest.
3. Compute the new balance forward. Add the previous balance and this month's interest, and subtract the payment.

A single formula for these steps is shown in Figure 7–2.

You can prove this formula by trying it with the example of paying $200 per month against a balance of $4,500, assuming an annual interest rate of 19.5 percent.

In this case:

$$F \text{ (previous balance)} = \$4,500$$
$$P \text{ (monthly payment)} = \$\ 200$$

FIGURE 7–2
Formula: Loan Amortization

$$F = B - \left[P - \left(B \times \frac{r}{12} \right) \right]$$

F = new balance forward
B = previous balance
P = monthly payment
r = annual rate

$$r \text{ (annual interest)} = 19.5\%$$

The annual rate is used in the formula in decimal form, so it shows up as .195 rather than as 19.5 percent. This figure is divided by 12 to arrive at the monthly rate.

Applying the formula:

$$F = 4{,}500 - \left[200 - \left(4{,}500 \times \frac{.195}{12} \right) \right]$$

$$= 4{,}500 - \left[200 - \left(4{,}500 \times .01625 \right) \right]$$

$$= 4{,}500 - \left[200 - 73 \right]$$

$$= 4{,}500 - \left[127 \right]$$

$$= 4{,}373$$

Apply the same steps to the second month, replacing 4,500 with the new balance, 4,373. The answer at the end of the second month will be 4,244. Both ending balances agree with the amounts shown on the amortization schedule on page 110.

Calculate loan amortization based on the amount you can afford to pay. Then you will be able to calculate how long it will take to eliminate the debt on your credit card. Stop using that card until you have completely wiped out the debt. Otherwise, you will be replacing budgeted debt reduction with new debt each month.

THE SCISSORS CURE

Let's assume that you follow all of the budgeting advice and planning steps we have outlined; that you try the reserve method to control credit card debt; and that you try to stop using your card—but your balance just stays where it was originally, and you can't seem to escape the cycle.

In that case, take the scissors cure. Cut up the card and throw it away. Contact the company, in writing, and cancel the card so that you won't be able to use it any more. Then budget your payments each month and make them until the debt is wiped out. Also recognize the fact that if you experience a problem staying with your plan, you probably shouldn't even use a credit card. It just destroys your efforts in reducing debt.

Overcome the misconception that there is a special value in having a line of credit. If you're able to keep it under control and use it in an appropriate way, there is nothing wrong with having one or more revolving credit accounts. But if you cannot follow your plan, the card is just getting in your way.

In the long run, you give up nothing when you cancel an account, except the temptation to overspend. You will be much better off controlling and planning your money so that you can stay in budget and out of debt.

Even when you have brought debts under control and you have escaped the debt syndrome, you may be prevented from using debt wisely if your credit rating is poor. The next chapter explains how credit bureaus work and summarizes your credit rights under the law.

CHAPTER 8

BIG BROTHER

People who are only good
with hammers see every
problem as a nail.
—*Abraham Maslow*

The credit bureau, it might seem, knows more about you than
anyone else. They are in the business of gathering information
about your finances, job history, and personal lifestyle. When
lenders or credit card companies receive your application, their
first step is to get a credit report. If there is anything negative
on that report, right or wrong, your application will probably
be rejected.

About 100 million Americans have negative information in
their credit files, including instances of late or past due payments; disputes with lenders; excessive credit; an unstable work
history; or any number of other notations and coded comments
that affect your ability to obtain credit.

The credit bureaus are subject to a number of laws that
protect you and your rights. In this chapter we will explain
how credit bureaus work, what's in your file, how to settle disputes, and how to protect your rights.

HOW CREDIT BUREAUS WORK

If you could wipe out all of your debts and never go into debt
again, having a clean credit record might not seem too important. But even if you are eventually able to get out of debt and

stay there, you should still be very concerned about what the credit agencies know about you, and whether or not their information is correct.

For example, you might want to buy a home in the future, meaning you will apply for a mortgage loan. Or you might be interviewed for a new job, and your would-be employer may send away for a credit report. In these instances, derogatory information could prevent you from getting the house or the job you want, even if you don't intend to apply for a new credit card, bank loan, or department store revolving account.

Credit agencies handle a massive volume of information, and they do make mistakes. Your credit report might include past due debts that aren't yours, or that were entered by mistake after you returned defective merchandise. Or, because an employee at the credit bureau hit the wrong button on a computer terminal, your current accounts might be rated past due or defaulted. Errors can affect you for many years. Any derogatory information will stay in your file for as long as seven years (bankruptcy information remains as long as 10 years).

The function of credit bureaus is often misunderstood. They supply information to banks, stores, employers, lenders, and others who request credit reports. They do *not* rate your credit, they only supply information. So a rejected application might arise because someone at your bank misinterprets the report they receive.

A credit report will contain information about you even when you have made payments on time. That is part of your credit history, just as past due or defaulted accounts are. But that doesn't mean that one credit agency will have your complete history. There are a number of agencies in the business, and a particular creditor might not have sent information to all of them. There are five major agencies operating in the United States, and most of them will have most of the major credit information about you.

Your credit history begins the first time you apply for credit. The first creditor sends information on your application to one or more of the agencies. From that point on, any time you apply for additional accounts or loans, your file is updated.

The five major agencies and their offices are:

TRW Credit
Alaska, Arizona, California, Colorado, Connecticut, District of Columbia, Florida, Georgia, Hawaii, Idaho, Illinois, Maryland, Massachusetts, Michigan, Montana, Nevada, New Mexico, New Jersey, New York, Ohio, Oregon, Pennsylvania, Rhode Island, South Carolina, Texas, Utah, Virginia, Washington, West Virginia, Wyoming.

Credit Bureau, Inc./Equifax
Alabama, California, Connecticut, District of Columbia, Florida, Georgia, Idaho, Maryland, Mississippi, Montana, New York, North Carolina, South Carolina, Virginia.

Chilton Corp.
Arizona, Arkansas, Colorado, Hawaii, Iowa, Louisiana, Maine, Massachusetts, Michigan, Minnesota, Nebraska, New Hampshire, New Mexico, New York, Oklahoma, Rhode Island, Tennessee, Texas, Vermont, Wyoming.

Trans Union Credit
Alabama, Alaska, Arkansas, California, Colorado, Connecticut, Delaware, Florida, Idaho, Illinois, Indiana, Kansas, Kentucky, Maine, Maryland, Michigan, Mississippi, Missouri, Montana, Nebraska, Nevada, New Jersey, New Mexico, New York, North Dakota, Ohio, Oregon, Pennsylvania, South Dakota, Tennessee, Utah, Washington, West Virginia, Wisconsin, Wyoming.

Associated Credit
Illinois, Indiana, Iowa, Kansas, Louisiana, Minnesota, Missouri, North Carolina, North Dakota, Ohio, Oklahoma, South Carolina, South Dakota, Tennessee, Texas, Virginia, West Virginia.

The offices of the five major bureaus are not limited to gathering information about people just in their states of operation. Because we buy so much over telephones and through catalogs, or obtain credit cards and bank loans across state lines, credit information is gathered and reported nationally. And for the same reasons, the federal laws affecting credit bureaus, creditors, and consumers are of greater interest than state and local laws.

CORRECTING ERRORS ON YOUR REPORT

What can you do when you apply for credit and it's rejected? For example, you are current on all debt payments, you have no disputes, and your credit history is clean. But when you apply for a credit card, your application is rejected, and, you're informed, the rejection was based on a credit report.

At this point, your first impulse may be to try and reason with the company that rejected your credit. Perhaps you could explain the circumstances or argue that the report is wrong, but this will not do much good. The company depends on the information supplied by the credit agency, and if there's an error on the report, you need to go through the agency and have the error corrected. Then you can reapply for credit.

Some typical errors that could end up on your credit report include:

- Debts that are not yours.
- A current account reported as past due.
- An unpaid debt for merchandise you returned or refused, or never received.
- A portion of a bill that's an overcharge and was not paid.
- Amounts resulting from math errors.
- An outstanding balance that you paid.
- Coding errors at the credit bureau.

You can request a copy of your credit report any time you want. If you make this request just to review the status of the report, the credit bureau will charge a fee. But if you have recently been rejected for credit, you have the right to get a free copy of your report. You must make the request within 30 days after receiving notice that credit has been turned down.

Send a letter to the credit bureau (the company rejecting credit will include the credit bureau name and address in their notification to you). Ask for a copy of your current credit report, and include the following information: Your full name, current address, addresses for the last five years (with dates), your social security number, and the name of the company that rejected your application. You must also sign the letter.

When you receive the credit bureau's report, examine it and verify all of the information reported. The status of your accounts will be coded, and the meaning of those codes are explained on the reverse side of the report or on an accompanying sheet. If you find an error, write to the credit bureau and explain why it is wrong. It's important to communicate at every stage in writing, so that you can ensure the credit bureau complies with the laws affecting them.

The credit bureau must investigate your dispute within a reasonable length of time. If they discover that their information is incorrect or if they cannot verify what is shown in their files, the information must be deleted. If you are advised that the error was found, write and ask how long it will take to correct your file. When that period of time has expired, ask for an updated copy of your report, to ensure that the correction was made.

Once the credit bureau has corrected your file, you should reapply for credit. The bank, store, credit card company, or other creditor will review your application again. If the disputed information was the cause for rejecting your original application, you will probably be granted credit. However, if there are other reasons (such as a history of verified past due balances), your application could be rejected again.

RESOLVING DISPUTES

When an account becomes past due, your credit report will show that fact—for as long as seven years. A single instance of late payment could harm your ability to obtain credit, even when you did eventually pay the creditor. The same procedure applies when an account is assigned to a collection agency. Even though you may eventually pay off the entire amount of debt, your credit report will still be derogatory.

Be aware that credit information is passed along to a credit bureau. When you have an outstanding balance and plan to pay it off, contact the creditor (in writing), and negotiate terms for repayment. Those terms should include a promise from the creditor to notify the credit bureau and have the negative information removed.

You should get this promise in writing. Otherwise, you have to prove that the creditor promised to have the derogatory information removed from your file. Since creditors are probably more interested in getting payment than in your future credit status, most will be willing to agree to these terms, as long as you do pay your bill as promised.

For example, a department store assigned your past due account to a collection agency. You have a plan to pay the entire debt over the next six months, but you also will want the negative entry removed from your credit file. Follow these steps:

1. Propose a repayment plan to the creditor or collection agency. As a condition of the plan, ask for a letter promising to remove derogatory information from your credit bureau file.
2. Make all payments on time, based on the schedule you have promised to keep.
3. Ask the creditor how long it will take to have the derogatory information removed from your file.
4. When that period has expired, write to the credit bureau and ask for an updated copy of your credit report. Make sure the creditor had the derogatory entry removed.
5. If the item is still on your report, write to the creditor and ask for immediate action. Remind the creditor that you have a written promise, and enclose a copy (not the original) of that letter.
6. If the creditor refuses to honor the agreement or doesn't act as promised, write to your state's Department of Consumer Affairs. Send a copy of your agreement with the creditor and a copy of your latest credit report. Briefly explain the problem, including dates. Send a copy of this correspondence to the creditor.

Creditors are subject to a number of laws protecting your rights. Credit bureaus must also comply with these laws. Be sure that all communication takes place in writing, even when you also make telephone calls or discuss credit problems in person.

CONSUMER CREDIT LAWS

A number of state and local laws will affect your credit rights and define the responsibilities of credit bureaus and creditors. However, federal laws are the most applicable, because interstate financial transactions are so common.

For example, you live in Maryland and buy merchandise in Delaware. The purchase is paid for on a credit card issued by a New York bank. You are supposed to receive delivery from a company in North Carolina. You do not pay your bill because you are overcharged, or the merchandise is damaged or not delivered. A negative report is sent to a credit bureau in New Jersey. Now, which state's laws would apply? In situations like this, federal laws define your rights and the responsibilities and liabilities of creditors and credit bureaus.

When corresponding with creditors and credit bureaus, cite applicable laws. Doing so informs the other side that you are aware of your rights, which are defined by the following federal laws:

Fair Credit Reporting Act

This law explains your rights as a credit consumer; it lists the procedures credit bureaus must follow and the disclosures they must make.

Of special interest is Title VI, Section 611. Paragraph (*a*) of that Section explains the rules for disputed information in your credit file. The credit bureau *must* investigate a disputed entry within a reasonable length of time. If an error is found or the original information cannot be verified, the negative entry must be removed from your file.

Title VI, Section 612 explains that you have the right to a free copy of your credit report if your application for credit has been rejected. To get a free copy you must request it within 30 days after being notified of the rejection.

You also have the right to get a copy of your report at any time. The credit bureau can charge you a fee for providing the report, but they must notify you in advance concerning the amount they will charge.

Truth in Lending Law

This law states that creditors must inform you of the total cost of borrowing, including the total amount of interest and other charges, such as service fees, appraisal fees, and any other charges added to interest. The total of finance charges is reported as the Annual Percentage Rate (APR). Comparing the total cost by percentage and amount, you will be able to select the most favorable financing terms.

Truth in Leasing Law

Leasing companies must disclose the costs and terms of leasing personal property (cars, appliances, furniture). This law applies for all leases that will run four months or more. Leasing companies must tell you the amount of monthly payments, security deposits, license fees, taxes, and maintenance charges.

The company is also required to tell you, in writing, your responsibility for insurance, maintenance, options to buy, and any balloon payments at the end of the lease term. You also have the right to get an independent appraisal (at your cost). If the lease does include a balloon payment, it cannot be greater than three times the average monthly payment.

Real Estate Settlement Procedures Act

This law requires mortgage lenders to disclose settlement (closing) costs when you buy a house. The law may not apply to all lenders or properties. For more details about this law, write for information to:

RESPA Office
Department of Housing and Urban Development
451–7th Street, S.W., Room 4100
Washington, DC 20410

Equal Credit Opportunity Act

Under terms of this law, no creditor or lender can discriminate against you on the basis of race, color, age, sex, or marital status.

The law also describes the types of information that creditors or lenders may *not* use in reviewing your application. For example, you cannot be rejected because you are on public assistance, or because you are a woman who might become pregnant and have to leave her job.

Fair Credit Billing Act

This act sets down the procedures that must be followed by creditors in correcting billing errors. For example, you receive a monthly bill from a department store. It may contain a number of errors:

- Charges for purchases you didn't make.
- The wrong amount.
- The wrong purchase date.
- A charge without sufficient explanation.
- Your payments not shown on the bill.
- Math errors.
- Charges for merchandise you returned or did not accept.

In any of these instances, you should notify the creditor, in writing, within 60 days from receipt of the bill. Include the following information:

- Your full name.
- Account number.
- Explanation of the error.
- Amount of the error.

You should pay the portion of the bill that is not in dispute. The creditor is required under this law to acknowledge your letter within 30 days. While the matter is under investigation, you cannot be charged interest or finance charges on the disputed amount. Within 90 days a correction must be made, or, if the billing is correct, an explanation must be given to you.

Electronic Fund Transfer Act

This law describes the rules for banks and savings institutions that allow you to make recurring payments by bank draft or provide you access to automated teller machines.

Institutions must provide you with the following information:

- Notice of your liability if an ATM card is lost or stolen.
- A phone number to use for reporting lost or stolen cards.
- A description of the procedures to be used for resolving disputes.
- The institution's business days.
- The types of fund transfers you are allowed to make, including any dollar limits.
- Charges assessed for electronic fund transfers.
- Your right to receive written documentation of electronic fund transfers.
- The procedure for stopping payments of preauthorized transfers.
- The institution's liability to you if it fails to stop transfers you request.
- Conditions under which the institution will give out your account information to third parties.

In the event you run into a dispute that cannot be settled by exchanging letters, you may need to write to regulatory agencies (addresses given at the end of this chapter) or even to hire an attorney.

FILING BANKRUPTCY

Some people think of bankruptcy as a convenient way to erase past debts and get a fresh start. The increase in personal bankruptcy petitions during recent years proves this point: About half a million people file each year.

Bankruptcy should be thought of only as a last resort, a step to take when every other avenue has been exhausted. This should be your attitude for a number of reasons:

1. Bankruptcy doesn't solve debt problems. **To really take charge of your finances, you need to change spending habits and create a workable plan.** You may file bankruptcy only to end up in trouble again within a year or two.
2. When you file bankruptcy, your credit report carries the information for as long as 10 years, making it very difficult to obtain credit at any level.
3. Bankruptcy doesn't necessarily wipe out your debts. One form of bankruptcy only reschedules your payments, a type of enforced budgeting.
4. You cannot escape some forms of obligation through bankruptcy, often those representing the greatest source of problems. These include tax liabilities, alimony, child support, student loans, and punitive damages.

There are two types of bankruptcy filed by individuals. They are Chapter 7 bankruptcy and Chapter 13.

Chapter 7

This is a complete discharge of debts. You are required to surrender your assets for liquidation and payment to creditors, through a bankruptcy estate.

Certain limitations are placed on what you have to give up, including up to $7,500 in home equity; one motor vehicle worth no more than $1,200; personal property with no one item valued above $200; jewelry worth $500 or less; professional tools up to $750 value; and an additional $400 plus any unused portion of your homestead exemption. (If you do not own a home, you may add the $400 and the $7,500.) Many states place a limit on exemptions you can claim when filing a Chapter 7 petition.

Chapter 13

This is an adjustment of debts of an individual with regular income. You agree to a repayment plan and keep your assets. A portion of your debts are paid from future income, based on a schedule over three to five years. In other words, a budget is imposed on you, and you must live within that budget.

Considering what bankruptcy does to your credit and, as a consequence, to your financial freedom, it should not be thought of as an alternative. Unless you are so hopelessly indebted that there is no other way out, bankruptcy is too drastic, and it will prevent you from obtaining any significant credit for many years to come.

To find out more about bankruptcy, write to:

American Financial Services Association
1101 Fourteenth Street, N.W.
Washington, DC 20005

Ask for the pamphlet, "What You Should Know Before Declaring Bankruptcy."

REBUILDING YOUR CREDIT

If your debt problems have been so severe that credit card companies, department stores, and other lenders will not do business with you, it's still possible to rebuild your credit rating. You might have to accept the fact that your record will have blemishes on it for as long as seven years; but even in the worst case, you can start to rebuild. Consider these steps:

1. Meet with your local banker and ask for the chance to establish a dependable credit record. Offer to place $500 in a savings account and pledge that account as collateral against a $500 loan, with payments over one year. A fully amortized loan at 12 percent will cost you $44.43 per month. The purpose of the loan is strictly to rebuild credit. The bank faces no risk, because your savings account secures it. You establish a history of making loan payments on time each month, and discharging the debt.

2. Apply for a collateralized credit card. Several institutions offer this. You are given a credit limit equal to the amount of money you pledge as collateral. For example, you put $500 in collateral into an account with the institution, and your credit card is approved with a $500 limit.

3. Establish new credit at a department store by agreeing to a very low purchase limit. With your past record in mind, the store may reject your application at first. But if you meet with the credit manager and explain that you want to rebuild, you may be able to reach an agreement. For example, you may agree to a credit limit of $100 and promise to pay the entire balance each month. These terms will extend for one year, after which the manager will review your account and consider raising the limit and relaxing repayment terms.

4. Make a purchase on the layaway plan. The store holds the merchandise and you begin a series of installment payments. By proving that you are able to keep to the schedule over three months or more, you establish the fact that you can plan ahead and keep your promises. Afterwards, the store might be willing to grant you limited credit.

5. For existing debts, negotiate with your creditors and try to arrange a rescheduled payment plan. This will relieve your monthly budget and keep you current, avoiding the past due status on your credit report. You may even be able to talk a lender into reversing a negative entry on your credit report for as long as you keep up the rescheduled payment plan.

6. Apply for a secured loan. Because the lender will be able to repossess your purchase if you don't continue your payments, there is less risk involved. And as long as you do make your payments on time, you will reestablish credit. A good example of this is an auto loan. Even if you've had poor credit in the past, an auto dealer will usually be able to find a lender for you. Of course, the interest rate on such a loan may be very high, but that's part of the cost of rebuilding credit. You may have to accept the high rate just to begin rebuilding.

7. Apply for a debit card. You will recall that this looks like a credit card and is used for purchases in the same way. There is a big difference, though. A credit card purchase is an advance which you repay. A debit card purchase is paid by deducting the amount from your savings or checking account balance. While this isn't quite the same as having a revolving line of credit, responsible use of a debit card does establish a responsible spending pattern.

8. Seek credit counseling. Do not work with any company that charges a fee and promises to fix your credit or clean up your credit status. No one but you can fix a negative report. Work with a Consumer Credit Counseling Service, which is a nonprofit agency. To contact one in your area, write to:

National Foundation for Consumer Credit
8701 Georgia Avenue, Suite 601
Silver Spring, MD 20910
Phone: (301) 589-5600

Request two pamphlets:

"National Foundation for Consumer Credit"
"Consumer Credit Counseling"

CONSUMER ASSISTANCE

The federal credit laws are designed to protect you from abuse and to ensure that you receive fair treatment from creditors, lenders, and credit bureaus. But if you cannot get satisfaction by corresponding with these agencies and companies, you may file a complaint with the regulatory agency responsible for compliance with federal law and with industry procedures.

Complaints concerning banks that are chartered by the Federal Reserve system should be directed to the central bank office:

Director
Division of Consumer and Community Affairs
Board of Governors
Federal Reserve System
Washington, DC 20551

You may also direct complaints or inquiries to the district bank in your area. Write to the Federal Reserve Bank at:

104 Marietta Avenue	600 Atlantic Avenue
Atlanta, GA 30303	Boston, MA 02106
P.O. Box 834	P.O. Box 6387
Chicago, IL 60690	Cleveland, OH 44101
400 S. Akard Street	925 Grand Avenue
Dallas, TX 75222	Kansas City, MO 64198

250 Marquette Avenue
Minneapolis, MN 55480
P.O. Box 66
Philadelphia, PA 19105
P.O. Box 442
St. Louis, MO 63166

33 Liberty Street
New York, NY 10045
P.O. Box 27622
Richmond, VA 23219
P.O. Box 7702
San Francisco, CA 94120

For complaints or inquiries concerning national banks, write to:

Comptroller of the Currency
Consumer Affairs Division
Washington, DC 20219

For matters involving interstate credit, write to:

Office of Proceedings
Interstate Commerce Commission
Washington, DC 20523

For credit questions and complaints involving mortgage bankers, consumer finance companies, and other creditors, write to:

Federal Trade Commission
Equal Credit Opportunity
Washington, DC 20580

You may also contact your state's Consumer Affairs Department for additional help in resolving credit and compliance problems.

A number of informative publications will help you to learn more about your credit rights and the laws affecting creditors and credit bureaus:

Consumer Information
P.O. Box 100
Pueblo, CO 81002

	"Consumer Information Catalog"	free
425R	"Buying and Borrowing: Cash in On the Facts	.50
587R	"Choosing a Credit Card"	free
426R	"Fair Credit Reporting Act"	.50
427R	"Fair Debt Collection"	.50

Publication Services
Division of Support Services
Board of Governors
Federal Reserve System
Washington, DC 20551

"Consumer Handbook to Credit Protection Laws"

"What Truth in Lending Means to You"

"How to File a Consumer Credit Complaint"

"The Equal Credit Opportunity Act and Age"

"The Equal Credit Opportunity Act and Women"

"The Equal Credit Opportunity Act and Doctors, Lawyers, Small Retailers"

"The Equal Credit Opportunity Act and Credit Rights in Housing"

"Fair Credit Billing"

"Truth in Leasing"

"If You Use a Credit Card"

"Alice in Debitland: Consumer Protections and the Electronic Fund Transfer Act"

Understanding how credit bureaus and the credit process works will help you to be a more informed, aware consumer. It will also help you when you do apply for credit or a bank loan. The next chapter explains how banks review loan applications, and how to work with a loan officer.

CHAPTER 9

YOUR FRIENDLY LOAN OFFICER

A financier is a pawnbroker
with imagination.
—*Arthur Wing Pinero*

You have probably heard the saying, "Banks will lend you money only when you don't need it." There is some truth in this, because lenders look at the risk of lending from a point of view that's very different from most borrowers'. The lower the bank's risks, the more willingly it will make a loan.

Your goal is to get out of debt and to avoid going back into debt in the future. There are instances, though, when you will need to work with a loan officer. For example, you may need to purchase a new car or apply for a mortgage loan on a home. It's not realistic to expect to live completely debt-free, but it is possible to go into debt as part of a plan and without losing control over your financial situation.

THE RISK FACTOR

A lot of people think of the loan officer as an all-powerful figure, who can decide at a whim to approve or to disapprove a particular application. Because you are not always told *why* your loan application was turned down, the perception is reinforced. But in fact, the bank (or other lender) goes through a predictable formula in its review. Loan officers may depend a little on instinct, but more weight is given to the financial facts gathered during the application process.

The bank reviews your application, credit report, and financial history with a few basic questions in mind:

- Can you afford the repayments on the loan, based on your income and other obligations?
- Have you repaid previous debts on time?
- What is your financial status today, including current income as well as current debts?

These questions all boil down to one all-important question:

*What is the risk—to the bank—that
you might not repay the loan?*

Remember, lenders want to put loans on their books. That's the business they're in. Without loan business they don't make a profit, and they won't be able to afford to stay in business. But at the same time, they want to take on the least amount of risk possible. If they grant a loan and it isn't repaid, they lose money.

The bank marks up the cost of money it handles. For example, banks encourage people to save by offering 6 percent on a passbook account. That money is loaned out at 9, or 10, or 11 percent. The difference between what they pay and what they charge is called *the spread.*

The spread must be large enough to cover the bank's operating expenses as well as the occasional default. In addition, the bank factors in enough spread to produce a net profit. The rate must also be competitive. If other lenders are charging 9 percent for loans and your bank wants 14 percent, it won't get much business—unless it assumes more risk than other banks and is willing to suffer more defaults. You may find a lender who will grant you easy credit—but you will also pay a much higher rate of interest.

The risk factor, from the bank's point of view, is no different than the risks faced by other businesses. A retail merchant marks up goods at a level adequate to make a profit, allowing for overhead, pilferage, and profit. But prices must still be competitive with the prices charged by similar stores. Insurance companies charge varying premiums for policy coverage based on their expectation of future benefit payments and desired profits. And a mail order company bases its prices on the cost it pays for merchandise, advertising and mailing expenses, and profit. The same rules apply to all businesses.

Some people think of banks as service organizations. They forget that the bank is a business that exists to make a profit and that bases its policies and decisions on the risks it faces.

Remembering that a bank is a business will help you to better prepare for the process of submitting an application. If you are aware of the risks from a banker's point of view, you will be able to address those risks and evaluate your financial status—even before you ask for a loan. The bank also operates by the profit motive. It does not want to lend money to someone who won't repay it.

THE LOAN APPLICATION

The mystery associated with the lending process is based only in part on not understanding how risk enters the decision to approve or disapprove. Financial institutions have created an image of dignity, as though they are above the motives of the common merchant. Lenders, in fact, *are* money merchants. They will grant a loan for a price (interest); but they will do all they can to reduce risks and to deal only with those borrowers who are most likely to continue the repayment schedule. Thus the idea that "they will lend you money only when you don't need it" is partly true.

This image is encouraged by the idea that you apply—or ask for—a loan. This procedure places the bank in a superior position. They can agree to make a profit from lending you money, or they can decline your application.

If you have no debts, a high income, and no history of financial problems, your bank will gladly lend you the money you want. On the other hand, why should the bank lend money to someone who probably cannot afford the payments? Their defaults will grow, payments will be delayed, and the bank's profits will fall.

Your future dealings with a bank should be coordinated with your goal of eliminating existing debt and then avoiding future debt problems. You won't let credit card balances creep upward to the point that your monthly payments are a burden and you have no credit limit remaining; you will spend money based on a monthly budget; and you will begin executing a plan to reach your long-term goals.

Those long-term goals might include buying a home, for example. Chances are, you will need to apply for a very substantial loan. The lender will be willing to grant that loan only if you are a low-risk borrower, meaning you have control over your debts, no current history of delayed payments, and a healthy relationship between income and monthly payment levels.

WHAT THE BANK LOOKS FOR

What happens when you fill out a loan application and submit it to your bank? What does the loan officer look for, and how does he or she decide whether to approve or to disapprove your request?

The information on the loan application includes both personal and financial information, including:

- Name and current address.
- Addresses for the past few years.
- Social security number.
- Marital status and number of dependents.
- Employer's name and length of employment.
- Jobs held for the past few years.
- Monthly income from all sources.

In addition, the application has space to write down all of your debts, including total amounts owed and monthly payments. These questions are used in several ways:

1. Collectively, it paints a picture of the kind of person you are. Are you employed and stable, earning a living and supporting a family? Or, do you move from one job to another, with gaps of unemployment in between?

2. The information is used to get a current credit report from one of the credit bureaus operating in your area. That report will show your financial history, allowing the bank to do two things: evaluate the pattern of your financial life, including the level of debt you carry; and compare the debts you list on your application to what the credit bureau says you owe.
3. The level of your existing debts, compared to income, tells the bank how well you can manage to repay a new loan. For example, if your current payments already place a strain on your monthly budget, a new loan might be too much. You wouldn't be able to afford to make monthly payments, and the bank's risks will be higher than if you can easily afford to make repayments.
4. The size of your family helps the bank determine what you must pay each month for food, clothing, utilities, maintenance, medical bills, and insurance.

Loan application forms vary in the detail level, but all lenders will want to gather enough personal information to ask for a current credit report and evaluate your job status, family size, and financial stability. Two important sections of the application are the balance sheet and monthly payment schedule.

The balance sheet is a listing of everything you own (your assets) and everything you owe (your liabilities, or debts). The total of assets, minus the total of liabilities, is your net worth. A simplified balance sheet is shown in Figure 9–1.

The first three lines show your liquid assets—cash, savings, and investments. Liquid assets include cash and other assets that can be easily converted to cash. The bank will compare your liquid assets to the total of your current debts. These are debts you must repay within the next 12 months. The bank multiplies your monthly payments by 12 to arrive at this total. Current debts include credit card and department store debt, loans from finance companies, automobile loans, and home mortgage or rent payments. If, in the bank's opinion, your liquid assets are insufficient for the level of current debt, you are considered a poor risk. The higher your liquid assets and the lower your current debt, the less risk the lender will assume by grant-

FIGURE 9–1
Personal Balance Sheet

Personal Balance Sheet

Name _____ Date _____

Assets:
    Cash – checking $ _____
    Cash – savings   _____
    Investments   _____
    Auto(s)   _____
    Business equity   _____
    Home market value   _____
    Other

    _____   _____
    _____   _____

    Total Assets $ _____

Liabilities:
    Credit card balances $ _____
    Auto loan(s)   _____
    Home mortgage balance(s)   _____
    Other

    _____   _____
    _____   _____

    Total Liabilities $ _____

    Net Worth $ _____

ing you a new loan. In other words, if you don't have enough income to afford all of your current debts plus payments on a new loan, your application will not be approved.

You cannot list balances in retirement accounts under assets. For example, you have contributed money to an Individual Retirement Account (IRA) each year. Under the rules for deferring taxes on these deposits, the amount cannot be listed as an asset or pledged as collateral on a loan.

You also cannot list federal savings bonds and other nontransferrable assets as security for loans. Savings bonds are issued to the purchaser directly and cannot be transferred to anyone else. They can be cashed in only by the original buyer.

Besides liquid assets—cash and investments—your assets also include illiquid assets such as your automobiles, equity in your own business, and the current market value of your home. The bank is interested in these items not only to determine your net worth, but also to see whether or not you have any assets that can be pledged as collateral.

The bank will prefer to give you a secured loan. You pledge assets as collateral, and in the event that you do not continue to make timely payments, the bank can seize those assets. A home mortgage loan is secured by the equity in your home, and an auto loan is secured by the value of the auto. If you don't make your payments, your home could be foreclosed, or your auto could be repossessed.

Banks also grant unsecured loans, but only to those borrowers with very strong financial status. They also charge a much higher rate of interest, since their risk is greater. In the event of default, they cannot seize assets, but have to depend on their ability to collect from you eventually, perhaps using a collection agency and accepting a delay in getting their money.

The liability section of the balance sheet includes the outstanding balances (not the monthly payments, but the total amount you owe) of all of your current debts. The balances on all credit cards, auto and personal loans, your home mortgage, and other debts are listed here. The difference between total assets and total liabilities is your net worth.

Another important section of the loan application is the listing of your monthly payments. Here, each debt is identified by type (including the name of the lender) and by account number, total balance due, and monthly payment. An example is shown in Figure 9–2.

In this section, write down *all* of your debts for the past seven years, even those you have paid off completely. If necessary, refer to a more detailed schedule, type it up, and attach it to the application. Even if you have been delinquent on a past debt, include it in this section. The information will show up on your credit report, and it makes a poor impression on the lender if you leave out any financial information from your past.

FIGURE 9–2
Monthly Payments

Monthly Payments			
TYPE OF DEBT	ACCOUNT NUMBER	BALANCE	MONTHLY PAYMENT
credit cards:			
_____	_____	$ _____	$ _____
_____	_____	_____	_____
_____	_____	_____	_____
_____	_____	_____	_____
auto loan(s):			
_____	_____	_____	_____
_____	_____	_____	_____
home mortgage(s) or rent:			
_____	_____	_____	_____
_____	_____	_____	_____
other:			
_____	_____	_____	_____
_____	_____	_____	_____
_____	_____	_____	_____
Total monthly payments			$ _____

The lender performs a very important financial test based on this section. The total of your monthly payments for current debts and other obligations (like rent) is added to an estimate of other payments—for food, utilities, recreation, and clothing. A local lender will have a fairly good idea of what it costs you to live in your area, so calculating your true monthly payment burden is not difficult.

The test is a simple one, but it's critical to the question of whether or not you will get the loan. Can you afford payments on a loan? By comparing the total of your payments to your monthly income, the bank will be able to decide very easily whether or not you have the financial ability to make payments, or, to reduce the lender's risk.

DECIDING WHEN TO BORROW

The worst time to apply for a loan is when you are already deep in debt and unable to afford the current level of monthly payments. "But that's when I really need the money," you might say. The money might give you immediate relief, it's true. But remember, the bank will review your application with *their* risks in mind, and not in consideration of what you need right now. If the bank sees a pattern of ever-growing debt, they will be unwilling to advance more money to you. What you *need* is not the deciding factor; it's what the bank is willing to *risk* that really counts.

As part of the debt pattern, the bank will reason, you not only will have difficulty making payments on a new loan; chances are, your debts will also continue to grow. The reality is, you're usually better off reducing your current debts without borrowing more money, even if that will take longer. Once you can demonstrate to the bank that you are gradually gaining control over your personal financial situation, they will be more likely to approve your loan application. When you don't need the money as desperately, the bank's risk is also reduced.

The problem occurs, though, when you need to buy a new car because the old one has broken down; or when you need a loan to pay for medical expenses or other unexpected emergencies. This is the real and destructive aspect of being in debt. When a crisis comes up, you are unable to find the help you need at the moment—perhaps because you didn't plan ahead.

The ability to borrow money, not borrowing itself, is a type of personal asset, a form of insurance against future emergencies. It is also a convenience to be able to borrow when you need and want to. There is a very direct relationship between a bank's willingness to advance you the money you want and the degree of financial strength you possess. That relationship is inescapable. It isn't just the ability to borrow that reduces the bank's risk, but your net worth, the assets you can pledge as security for a loan, and the degree of control you exhibit over your finances.

Example: You own a home and are making payments on a mortgage loan. Equity has built up over several years. Now you want to add a fourth bedroom because your family is growing. The equity in your home will secure a home improvement loan.

Example: You have three credit cards and keep the balances current. Now you'd like to buy a new car. The bank reviews your application and grants the loan because your history shows no delay in payments and your total debt level is not excessive.

In these cases, a pattern of control means your chances of getting a loan are greatly improved, and approval might even be downright automatic. If you had used the equity in your home, through a second mortgage or an equity line of credit, to pay for an expensive vacation, to do Christmas shopping, or to buy a recreational vehicle, the equity would not be there to add another room. And if you owe many debts, including some that are past due, the bank might turn down your application for an auto loan.

DEBT CONSOLIDATION

We have argued against debt consolidation, even though many lenders encourage it. Consolidation may have some merit, though, assuming that you are able to establish a plan and a budget and stick to it. Too often, debt consolidation leads not to a solution, but to even greater problems.

Here's how it usually works. You owe money to a number of department stores, credit card companies, and the bank. The total comes to $6,000, and your monthly payments are $275. You apply for a loan at 11 percent interest, with the idea of consolidating the overall debt. Over a four-year period, a $6,000 loan will cost you about $155 per month, on a fully amortized basis (similar to a home mortgage).

The idea makes sense, on the surface. You will make only one payment per month, and the burden is reduced from $275 to $155. Several things may go wrong with the plan, however:

1. The extra $120 per month in your budget goes not into savings where it belongs, but to increasing your standard of living—on a permanent basis. You haven't really improved your financial situation, you've only shifted it and extended the repayment on your debt for a longer period of time.

2. Even though you pay off the balances of your previous debt, that debt returns within a year. Your credit card and department store balances rise. Now you have the new loan to repay, plus the additional debt from replacing credit card debt. In a few months you have used up your credit limit again.

3. The temporary relief you get from consolidation allows you to relax your diligence; thus, your budget is ignored and spending levels rise.

All of these consequences of debt consolidation keep you in debt and add to the problem. It's even possible that consolidation mistakes are repeated over and over, but at ever-growing dollar heights. The problem is not only a financial one. It's a recurring pattern of spending, the lack of a plan, and the lack of controls, that make consolidation a poor idea.

Consolidation can work to your advantage, but only if it's entered into with a plan and with rules you will enforce for yourself and for your family. Using the same example—a $6,000 debt and payments of $275 per month, to be replaced with a four-year loan and payments of $155 per month—these rules should include:

1. The $120 per month you save will go directly into savings, at the beginning of every month—without fail. This does not change your financial situation, because you've been making those $275 payments. Now, though, you will save part of it.

2. The prior debts will *not* be repeated. The credit cards should be put away, at least until the new debt has been paid off. If the temptation is too great, cut your cards in half and close your accounts.

3. Repayment of the consolidation loan will become a high-priority goal. You will resolve to avoid any additional debt until that loan has been repaid. And, if possible, you will avoid going into debt even after the loan has been repaid.

Consolidation makes sense only if you are able to use it as a technique for getting out of debt and staying out, while also increasing your personal savings. Avoid the common pattern of trying to achieve budget relief, only to find yourself in more trouble as a result.

One argument favoring consolidation is this: The bank will not grant you a loan if your monthly payments are too high, based on your income. Through consolidation, the debt repayment schedule is extended, and your monthly payments are lowered. Thus, you have a better chance of getting the loan. There's more money in your budget for those monthly payments.

This seemingly logical argument keeps you in debt and only leads to more problems in the future. The only real solution to debt problems is to pay off those debts. Yes, you can reduce monthly payments through consolidation; but you will stay in debt for a longer time, pay more interest to the lender, and risk increasing your liabilities—all of which are detrimental to your financial health.

LENDER PROMOTIONS

Many lenders encourage you to consolidate debts, even though they know about the risks you assume, and even when they believe consolidation will only make your problems worse. As long as the bank's consolidation loan is secured (by home equity, for example), their risks are low. In comparison, your own risk is quite high.

Example: Many lenders encourage homeowners to use the equity that's "sitting idle" in their home, as though the cash were buried in the basement. This makes you feel guilty for not taking advantage of the easy equity. But, in truth, using your equity is nothing more than taking out a loan—going into debt— and securing that loan with your home's equity, which is one of your most valuable assets. You place that equity at risk when you borrow money. You are not using your equity, you're jeopardizing it, especially if you use the proceeds to consolidate other debts, buy a car, or take a vacation. These uses of money do not increase your net worth. And borrowing money secured by home equity reduces your net worth. You're spending your assets to go further into debt when you secure your loan with equity.

Banks often push this idea based on the tax argument. Interest on a home mortgage (or a line of credit secured with home equity) is fully deductible, while other forms of interest are not. Thus, the argument goes, if you shift your debt burden into the deductible category, you get a tax deduction you lose otherwise.

It seems to make sense, but it really doesn't. For example, if your effective tax rate is 33 percent, you get a deduction of 33 cents for every dollar of interest you pay. You will be much better off getting completely out of debt and paying no interest at all. At the same time, you preserve the asset of home equity and avoid the cycle of debt.

It's in the bank's best interest, not yours, to keep debt alive. Banks, like credit card companies, are in the lending business. They depend on the interest you pay to stay in business. It's an easy formula: The more you pay in interest and the lower the bank's risks, the more profit they earn—and the longer you stay in debt.

Secured loans are very attractive to the bank. If a loan is secured by home equity, for example, the bank may lend money even to those who simply cannot afford repayments. When the loan is defaulted, the bank can foreclose, sell the house, and get its money back. And even if the borrower does somehow manage to make every payment, the bank earns a very respectable profit from the interest it gets.

Ultimately, the lender stands to make more profit from your purchase of a home than you do, even if your home equity grows substantially over many years. In the next chapter, we will explore the question of home mortgages and other long-term loans in more detail, and demonstrate how the debt cycle increases the real cost of buying a home.

CHAPTER 10

DEBTOR'S PRISON

Life is what happens when
you are making other plans.
—*John Lennon*

In the old days, those with unpaid debts were sent to debtor's prison—along with their entire families. In some cultures, the institution was called the Poor House, a slight improvement. You probably thought these medieval ideas died out many years ago, but in fact, we still have a type of Poor House today. It's a system that keeps us in debt for many years and, in some cases, prevents us from ever getting out of debt.

The modern debtor's prison is the long-term loan. When you buy a home, an expensive car, a recreational vehicle, or a boat, you may arrange financing over many years. In fact, due to compound interest, you end up paying for these purchases several times over. You can even refinance your purchase, so that the debt is turned over and you will pay even more interest. As a result, you are never released from debtor's prison.

For example, the real cost of buying a home is *not* the purchase price, but the amount paid to a lender over the mortgage term. With a 30-year mortgage, that cost can be substantially higher than the negotiated purchase price.

Example: You purchase a home for an agreed price of $100,000 and make a down payment of $20,000. With a 10 percent, 30-year mortgage, the real total cost of your home is $272,742.

If that $100,000 home is worth $272,000 after the mortgage is paid off, you will not have made any profit on the investment. The equity is earned by the lender through interest payments. Your home is worth more than the original purchase price, but you could have saved as much by putting the same money into a savings account.

Example: Instead of buying a $100,000 home, you deposit $833.33 each quarter in a savings account that pays 6 percent (compounded quarterly). After 30 years, your account is worth $276,072:

Savings Balance

Amount Invested	Interest	Total Value
$100,000	$176,072	$276,072

Why does the 6 percent savings account exceed the increased value of your home? The reason is that interest is compounded in your favor. Your savings grow at an ever-accelerating rate. When you're paying on a long-term debt, compounding works against you and in favor of the lender. So the rate of repayment is very slow during the early years and picks up only in the last six or seven years. Thus, the lender makes a greater profit than the homeowner.

A similar outcome takes place when you buy an automobile, or a boat, or a recreational vehicle. The longer the repayment term, the more you really pay for your purchase, and the more the lender earns by keeping you in debt.

THE HIDDEN COSTS

Your monthly budget will be affected in many ways when you enter a long-term loan agreement. This effect is often much greater than just the monthly payment. In order to stay in control of your expenses, evaluate your purchases with this point in mind.

Example: You have been renting for the last few years, and you are now considering buying your first home. A comparison of rent and mortgage payments (with tax benefits in mind) shows that you can afford to buy. But in addition to the mortgage payment, you will also need to budget for other expenses you didn't have as a renter. These include homeowner's insurance, maintenance, and higher utility expenses. These extras don't make the purchase a poor idea, but the on-going expense will be greater than when you were a renter.

Example: You own an economy car and want to trade it in on a luxury sports car that costs $24,000. You can afford the monthly payments, which the dealer says can be arranged over a seven-year period. The extra expenses will include much higher auto insurance, higher maintenance costs, registration and licensing fees, and a higher rate of interest in many cases. Some dealers offer low-interest incentives, but these usually apply to loans running three years or less. You might not be able to afford a short-term loan, so you'll be stuck with a higher interest rate. If you buy a high-profile car (like a small red sports car), you might also attract more attention from Smokey, meaning you'll be paying more for tickets. These will increase your auto insurance bill again.

Example: You finance a purchase of a sailboat, or a motorcycle, or an RV. These luxury items are financed with long-term loans. But in addition to the payments, you will pay for insurance, registration fees, and maintenance. Fuel costs may be high for boats and RVs offsetting any presumed economy. You may buy an RV to save on hotel bills while traveling, and end up paying much more in hidden costs than you save in lodging.

MANAGING YOUR MORTGAGE LOAN

The 30-year mortgage may be a permanent debt, and many homeowners may resign themselves to it. You may simply assume that it's inevitable, and there's nothing you can do about it. Or, you can look at the mortgage debt in another way. If you repay the loan at an accelerated rate, you achieve three benefits:

1. You accumulate equity in your home more rapidly than you would by staying with the contractual schedule.
2. You eliminate the debt more rapidly.
3. You determine and control the real cost of your home by converting less equity to the lender and keeping more for yourself.

In other words, the "permanent" mortgage debt does not have to be permanent. By building even a small amount of additional principal payment into your monthly budget, you can take quite a few years off the repayment term and reduce the interest expense at the same time.

Your home is a personal shelter, and the equity you build over the years should be carefully preserved and protected. You achieve this by maintaining your home, by paying for homeowner's insurance, and by leaving your equity intact. Remember, when you take out a new mortgage on your home, you are borrowing money secured by home equity. Using a home as a convenient line of credit prevents you from getting out of debt.

You can run into several problems in managing your mortgage. These include:

1. The real cost of borrowing is extremely high. You accumulate equity very slowly during the first few years in your home, while the lender makes a lot of money.
2. Lenders keep you in debt by making loans readily accessible through equity lines of credit. You're better off avoiding these, since they rarely help you to get out of debt and just work to keep you there.
3. Second mortgages are easy to get, as long as you have enough equity. But like lines of credit, seconds just increase your debt level and work against the idea of gaining equity and reducing debt.
4. Refinancing might seem like a good idea, and in some instances, you can reduce interest by replacement. But beware. If refinancing means extending the repayment date by several years, you will be in debt for a longer period, and you will pay much more in interest, too.

The solution is to devise a repayment plan and stick to it. This plan should be coordinated with your long-term financial goals. Of course, the more immediate problem of getting rid of credit card and short-term loan debts must take priority in your plan. But at the same time, you can begin to think about what you want to achieve in 10, 20, or 30 years.

Example: You would like to retire at the age of 60. In order to achieve this goal, you will need to eliminate your debts by that time. You are now 35 and have just purchased a home with a 30-year mortgage. The loan balance is $80,000 and the interest rate is 10 percent while monthly payments are $702.06.

Under the contractual schedule, the loan won't be repaid until you are 65. However, by increasing your monthly payment to $726.97 starting with the first month—an additional $24.91 per month—your loan will be paid in full in 25 years.

Later in this chapter, you'll see how to figure out the amount of payment needed to pay off a loan in fewer years. For now, the point is this: Your mortgage contract specifies the amount you are required to pay each month, but you can repay the loan at a faster rate.

Chances are, if you are a first-time homebuyer, you will be tied in to a 30-year schedule because you can't qualify for the higher payments of a shorter term. The lender evaluates your loan application by comparing the monthly payment to your monthly income. The longer the repayment term, the lower the payment. If the ratio is too steep, a lender simply won't approve the loan.

Another consideration is your monthly budget. If you are used to paying $400 per month in rent, mortgage payments of $700 would be a big jump in your budget. Agreeing to a shorter-term loan is out of the question.

These points don't mean you must stay with the original schedule, though. Once you have your home, you can increase the monthly payment and build that increase into your budget, even if it's only a small amount. That's a form of savings that pays a better rate of interest than most other investments.

METHODS OF BUILDING HOME EQUITY

There are three ways that a home grows in value. The first way is an increase in market value, which grows from demand in the area. When the population is on the rise, the price of homes grows at a corresponding rate. This is the most visible method by which an investment in a home pays off.

The second way is increased value resulting from improvements. For example, your home's living space can be increased by adding a second or third bathroom, or installing a deck and a swimming pool. The value of improvements is limited, however. The amount of profit you'll realize will depend to a large degree on the average sales price of other homes in the same area. Thus, over-improving a home may be desirable while you're living in it, but when you sell, you might not be able to recapture the entire investment.

The third way that your home grows in value is through the repayment of a mortgage loan. If you purchase a $100,000 home with $20,000 down, you owe the lender the balance of $80,000. Each dollar paid off on that loan increases your equity by the same amount. Here you have the most control, and you can accelerate the pace of equity while reducing the cost of buying.

Over a 30-year period, the rate of equity growth is painfully slow during the first few years because the interest is based on the outstanding balance of the loan. When the balance is high, most of your payment goes toward interest, and only a few dollars per month are assigned to principal—your equity.

Example: Assuming a mortgage of $80,000, to be repaid over 30 years at 10 percent, you will pay off only 3.4 percent of the loan during the first five years. For a total of more than $42,000 in mortgage payments, only $2,741 goes to principal. The rest is paid to the lender in interest. Since most first-time homebuyers stay in their homes only four to five years, that means very little equity is built up during the first five years.

Example: On the same loan, one-half of the total debt is still due after 23 years. From that point forward, most of the payments go toward principal. But over the whole 30-year period, your total payments will be higher than $252,000, more than 300 percent of the original mortgage amount.

The slow rate of repayment on a 30-year loan is illustrated in Figure 10–1. Note that the repayment line curves downward very slowly for most of the term and only picks up during the last few years.

The lender will make more profit on your home than you will, even if your home more than doubles in value during the 30 years. Even after the benefits of deducting interest on your tax return are considered, the real cost of your home is much higher than the purchase price. The aftertax interest expense

FIGURE 10–1
Remaining Balance Schedule

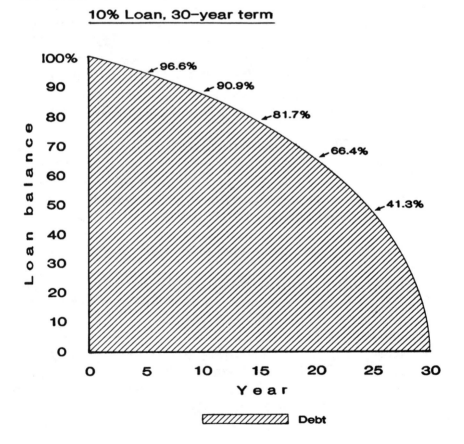

10% Loan, 30-year term

is shown on the following table, assuming that your tax rate is 33 percent each year (meaning that every dollar paid in deductible interest saves 33 cents in taxes):

The High Cost of Interest

	Purchase Price	Real Cost	Aftertax Cost
Down payment	$ 20,000	$ 20,000	$ 20,000
Mortgage	80,000	80,000	80,000
Interest	0	172,742	115,737
Total	$100,000	$272,742	$215,737

The deductibility of interest should be considered when you compare the cost of renting to the cost of home ownership. On an aftertax basis, the interest deduction is an important part of the real cost comparison. However, once you have purchased a home, the true cost of that purchase is high, but you can control it with a little budgeting and a little planning.

THE REAL COST OF A MORTGAGE

Even a modest increase in your monthly payment will greatly reduce the true cost of buying a home. You can and should tailor an acceleration program to suit your personal budget. For example, based on an $80,000 mortgage with a 30-year term at 10 percent interest:

- By making a single extra payment during the first month of a 30-year mortgage (thus, making 13 payments in the first year), you will reduce the total repayment term by one full year.
- By paying off a 30-year mortgage at a 15-year rate, you will save $97,990 in interest. The additional payment will be $157.63 per month.
- By paying an extra $100 per month, you will save $80,000 in interest (the original mortgage balance), and you will reduce the repayment period by 12 years.
- By paying an extra $25 per month, you will save $34,000

in interest, and you will reduce the repayment period by five years.

A similar program of acceleration works for variable-rate loans as well. In order to qualify for the level of required payments, some homeowners agree to a variable rate when they buy a home. The initial rate may be lower than the market rate, but within six months or so, it begins to climb. Over a number of years, the variable-rate loan may cost more than the fixed-rate loan.

Acceleration reduces the level of debt immediately. And, when a variable-rate loan's interest rate is increased, the lower outstanding balance also reduces the future payment, since the payment level will be based on the outstanding balance.

One method of accelerating a variable-rate loan is to make payments at a level equal to 1 percent above the required payment. Thus, if the loan starts with an 8 percent rate, payments are made at the level required to repay the loan as if the rate were 9 percent. Then, when the rate is increased to 9 percent, you increase your monthly payments to the 10 percent level.

A second method is to build an amount into your budget above the required payment, and stick to that amount each and every month. While a 1 percent increase in a variable-rate loan might not seem too drastic, consider what it means in terms of the required payment. For example, one variable-rate loan contract starts out at 8 percent. The lender may increase the rate by as much as 1 percent every six months, to a maximum of 13 percent. In two and one-half years that loan's payments could grow to the maximum. Based on an $80,000 mortgage with 30 years in the repayment term:

Monthly Payment

Interest Rate	Payment
8%	$587.02
9	643.70
10	702.06
11	761.86
12	822.90
13	884.96

If the maximum increase goes into effect, the additional strain on your budget would be nearly $300 per month. Any acceleration put into effect during the first few years in a variable-rate mortgage will certainly reduce the interest costs over time, as well as the total number of years required to repay the loan.

COORDINATING ACCELERATION WITH INCOME

The fixed-rate mortgage might cost more during the first 6 to 12 months; but after that, the variable-rate loan is likely to become more expensive. One of the greatest benefits of investing in your own home is the protection against inflation that's provided through a fixed-rate, long-term mortgage.

Example: You are committed to payments of $700 per month for the next 30 years. You currently take home about $2,500 per month, but you expect your income to increase over the course of your career. Since the mortgage level is fixed but your income is not, your mortgage payment will represent a decreasing percentage of income over time.

The same is not true when you pay rent. Chances are, as your income rises and as property values grow, so will your rent. Estimate your future income, and compare the fixed mortgage payment to see what percentage it is. Over time, the cost of housing actually declines:

Percentage of Income

Year	Monthly Income	Mortgage Payment	Percent
1	$2,500	$700	28
5	3,100	700	23
10	3,600	700	19

One way to accelerate your mortgage is to fix the percentage of your income that goes toward housing costs. In this example, you started out paying 28 percent of your income. If you can afford that level of payment today, you may be able to budget the same level each time your income goes up. So payments are increased to:

Percentage of Income

Year	Monthly Income	Mortgage Payment	Percent
1	$2,500	$ 700	28
5	3,100	868	28
10	3,600	1,008	28

This increase would not occur suddenly. It would be budgeted each time you receive a raise. The net effect will be gradual and won't create a strain. As an example of how this type of acceleration would work, let's assume that on average, you will increase your monthly payment by $50 at the beginning of each year. Under this plan, your $80,000, 10 percent loan will be paid off in less than 16 years. Total interest will come out to $82,016, a savings over full acceleration of $90,700. Thus, you eliminate the debt 14 years sooner and save a lot of money on interest—just by gradually increasing the monthly payment as your income goes up.

INFLATION AND YOUR MORTGAGE

When you are paying for your home under a fixed-rate mortgage, inflation is definitely on your side. Not only is the amount of your housing cost fixed, but you also have the opportunity to accelerate the rate of repayment without really affecting your budget.

To appreciate how even a low rate of inflation affects you over a number of years, you will need to review inflation from two sides. First, let's review buying power, the declining value of a dollar. As prices rise, a dollar won't go as far; thus, your buying power is affected, and the after-inflation value of a dollar is lowered.

The second side is cost. If you spend $100 per week on groceries, what will the same groceries cost you in five years? That depends on the rate of inflation. At an annual rate of 2 percent, those groceries will cost $110; at a 4 percent annual rate, you will spend $122.

Inflation affects the prices of homes, and also affects your housing costs. Figure 10–2 shows the two sides of inflation. First is buying power, the declining value of one dollar, based on annual rates of inflation. Second is cost, the growing level required to make purchases at different rates of inflation.

You can use both of these tables to figure out what you will pay for housing (whether rent or mortgage payments) over time; and to figure out how your take-home pay may or may not keep pace with inflation and the cost of housing.

FIGURE 10–2
Inflation-Adjusted Values

a: buying power

YEAR	INFLATION RATE		
	2%	3%	4%
0	1.00	1.00	1.00
5	.90	.86	.82
10	.82	.74	.66
15	.74	.63	.54
20	.67	.54	.44

b: cost

YEAR	INFLATION RATE		
	2%	3%	4%
0	1.00	1.00	1.00
5	1.10	1.16	1.22
10	1.22	1.34	1.48
15	1.35	1.56	1.80
20	1.49	1.81	2.19

You can build your own inflation tables with a calculator. The first table, buying power, involves dividing one by a series of inflation rates, one for each year. The steps on a calculator are:

1. Enter 1.
2. Depress the "divide" button.
3. Enter 1 plus the rate of inflation you assume for each year. (For example, if you assume 2 percent inflation, enter 1.02; if you assume 4 percent inflation, enter 1.04.)
4. Depress the "equals" button. This figure shows the buying power of one dollar after one year.
5. Depress the "equals" button again to find the buying power after two years. Repeat this for as many years as you want.

You can apply the inflation factor to identify your true housing cost over any number of years. By depressing the "equals" button 30 times, you will find the true cost of a mortgage by the end of your mortgage term, based on the assumptions you are using concerning the rate of inflation.

Example: Your mortgage payment is $702 per month. In after-inflation dollars, what will your payment equal after five years?

Referring to the buying power table, today's payment should be multiplied by the five-year factor. If you assume a 3 percent rate of inflation, that factor is .86:

$$.86 \times \$702 = \$603.72$$

To figure out the cost side of inflation, follow these steps:

1. The first year's cost is equal to 1, plus the rate of inflation you're using. For example, if you assume 2 percent inflation, the cost after the first year is $1.02 per dollar.
2. Enter 1 plus the rate of inflation you assume for each year.
2. Depress the "multiply" button.
3. Depress the "equals" button. This figure shows the cost factor at the end of the second year.
4. Depress the "equals" button once for each subsequent year.

You can use the cost calculation for several tests. If you apply an assumed rate of inflation to housing, you can figure an estimate of future home prices. If you believe your income will keep pace with inflation, the cost factors can be used to estimate future earnings.

Example: Today, the average three-bedroom home costs $85,000 in your area. If homes will increase in value by 4 percent per year (on average), what will the same home cost in five years?

Referring to the cost table, the 4 percent factor in five years is 1.22:

$$1.22 \times \$85,000 = \$103,700$$

Example: You currently earn $2,500 per month and assume that your wages will keep pace with inflation. If you believe inflation will average 3 percent per year, what will you earn in five years?

The cost table shows that the five-year factor in the 3 percent column is 1.16:

$$1.16 \times \$2,500 = \$2,900$$

With inflation in mind, it could be argued that buying a home today is an excellent investment, even if you pay for that home several times over through interest payments. But compare the cost of a home (assuming interest over the term of your mortgage) to the assumed increase in market value.

Example: You purchased a home for $100,000, financing $80,000 over 30 years at 10 percent. Assuming that inflation will average 3 percent per year, what will the home be worth by the time it's paid off?

We need to calculate the cost over 30 years, at an assumed rate of 3 percent per year:

$$(1.03)^{30} \times \$100,000 = \$242,726$$

The total of payments on the $80,000 mortgage will be $252,742. Added to the down payment of $20,000, you paid a total of $272,742, or $30,000 more than the inflated value of the home. But before completing the comparison, we must add in the tax benefit of deducting interest. Assuming you will be taxed at 33 percent each year, we must reduce the cost. Interest comes up to $172,742, so:

$$33\% \times \$172,742 = \$57,005$$

With the tax benefit in mind, the true profit on this home can now be calculated:

Market value after 30 years		$242,726
Total payments	$272,742	
Less: Tax benefits	− 57,005	
Aftertax payments		215,737
Net profit		$ 26,989

In this example, based on an assumed inflation rate of 3 percent, you—the homeowner—earn a profit of nearly $27,000. The lender, though, lends $80,000 and earns a profit of $172,742.

ACCELERATION AS AN INVESTMENT

You can reverse the obvious advantage the lender holds and earn a higher degree of return on your investment. You can control the rate of equity growth while reducing the repayment term.

Think of mortgage acceleration as an investment. The yield you earn is equal to the interest rate you're paying. So whenever you reduce total interest cost, you are earning money, just as you would by putting your money in the bank.

Lenders and financial advisers often argue against this plan, insisting that you can use your money better by investing it elsewhere. This might be true if you're only paying 6 percent on your mortgage. But most of us are paying at least 9 or 10 percent. It's very doubtful that you will be able to find an investment that beats that yield *and* provides you with the same degree of safety as your own home.

If you decide to look for an investment other than mortgage acceleration, consider these safety features:

- Your home investment is insured against loss through your homeowner's policy.
- You keep an eye on your investment every day and maintain its value by caring for your property.
- Every dollar put into principal today reduces interest costs for the remainder of your loan period; thus, acceleration produces a compounded rate of return.

The major disadvantage of mortgage acceleration is that the money you invest is difficult to retrieve. It is a very illiquid way to invest. With that in mind, it's critical that you build an emergency reserve fund—money you can get your hands on quickly in case you need it. Once you put extra money into paying off your mortgage debt, you can only get it back by taking out a new mortgage, or going back into debt.

READING INTEREST TABLES

In order to control your mortgage debt level and to plan ahead and identify a desired pay-off year, you will need to refer to interest amortization tables. These are rows and columns of numbers that tell you what your monthly payment will be, assuming different interest rates, numbers of years in the mortgage term, and the amount of the loan. Books of tables can be purchased in any bookstore for prices beginning at about $3.95.

One type of table shows the actual dollar amount required to amortize, or repay a loan. Columns are arranged to show the number of years, while rows report the monthly payment for various loan amounts. You can use this type of table to calculate a degree of amortization.

Example: Your loan was originally $80,000. You are paying over 30 years at the rate of 10 percent. Payments are $702 per month. At the end of the fifth year, your balance is about $77,000. You have 25 years to go, but you want to pay it off in 20 years.

Refer to the 10 percent table in an interest amortization book. Find the line for your current balance of $77,000, and find the row for 20 years. The required payment is $743. Thus, if you increase your monthly payment by $41 per month, you will reduce your term by five years.

With this type of interest amortization table, you may need to add two or more numbers together. The loan amounts are generally given in round numbers. Thus, for the payment of a $77,000 loan, you will need to add the payment for $75,000 to the payment for $2,000.

An alternative is to buy an interest table book that shows a factor rather than an amount. These books are divided into sections for monthly, quarterly, semiannual, and annual compounding. For a mortgage, you should refer to the tables for monthly compounding. In the 10 percent column, factors look like this:

Years	10 Percent
20	0.0096502
21	0.0095078
22	0.0093825
23	0.0092718
24	0.0091739
25	0.0090870
26	0.0090098
27	0.0089410
28	0.0088796
29	0.0088248
30	0.0087757

You can apply these factors in a number of ways. For example, to verify the fully amortized payment on the original loan, multiply the 30-year factor by the loan amount:

$$0.0087757 \times \$80,000 = \$702.06$$

To see what will be required to pay off the loan in a shorter period of time, multiply the appropriate factor by your current balance. The actual balance at the end of five years will be $77,259.23. You have 25 years remaining but want to know how much you will have to pay per month over the next 20 years. The 20-year factor for a 10 percent loan is 0.0096502:

$$0.0096502 \times \$77,259.23 = \$745.57$$

The factor table is easier to use than the dollar amount table, and it produces a more exact amount for you.

OVERCOMING THE MISCONCEPTIONS

Misconceptions about mortgage debt and the cost of housing prevent many people from accelerating their mortgage payments. By examining these misconceptions, you will be able to see the picture more clearly and to coordinate the reduction of long-term debt with your own future plans.

The first misconception is: *The cost of a home is the price you agree to pay.* As you've already seen, the real cost is the sum of your down payment, your loan balance, and interest. So when you repay a loan in 15 or 20 years instead of in 30, the cost will be much lower—perhaps as much as $100,000.

The second misconception is: *Fixed-rate mortgages protect you from inflation, so acceleration isn't necessary.* In fact, the cost of interest is so high that the lender will invariably earn the lion's share of inflated values on mortgaged property. You can change the ratio by accelerating your mortgage.

The third misconception is: *Your investment grows as the result of ever-growing market values.* The sad fact is, the interest you pay to the lender may well outpace the rate of inflation. And even if equity exceeds the interest cost, the lender makes more from your investment than you do.

The fourth misconception is: *You can find better investments outside of your home mortgage.* Even if you could exceed the compound yield represented by your home mortgage, don't overlook the need to compare risks. You are unlikely to find an investment that exceeds the rate you're paying on a mortgage of 10 percent that also provides the same degree of safety.

The fifth misconception is: *You shouldn't accelerate payments because doing so reduces your tax benefits.* This is the most outlandish of all the anti-acceleration arguments, yet it's cited most often. You will always come out ahead by reducing interest costs, even after taxes. For example, if you reduce your total interest expense by $100,000, you may lower your tax benefits by $33,000. But you will still be ahead by the difference: $67,000.

Accelerating your mortgage payment is a sound method for getting out of long-term debt. You may apply the same idea to eliminating credit card balances, simply by paying an amount that's higher than the required minimum. You saw previously how much you will save in interest.

WATCHING FOR THE DANGER SIGNALS

With any type of long-term loan, your goal should be to ensure that your plan dictates your actions. Don't go into debt without first studying the decision with the hidden costs in mind, and without understanding the consequences of taking on the debt.

Watch for these signs:

1. The tax benefits are emphasized. When a salesperson distracts you by saying you can write off the interest (such as on a home mortgage), remember that you're still paying a lot of money to the lender.

2. The affordability of payments becomes a bigger issue than the need for the debt. You should stop and think whenever you're in a dealer's showroom, and the salesperson asks you, "How much can you afford to pay each month?" This is *not* the important question to answer. The real question is, "Can I afford this purchase and the hidden costs that will come with it?" Another question you may ask is, "Would I be better off buying a more economical model?"

3. The action reduces equity. For example, you own a home and you have built up equity over the years. You receive an ad in the mail from your lender advising you that you're preapproved for refinancing and that you can have $35,000 just by making a phone call. Remember: If you needed that money, you would already be trying to get it. Don't respond to the temptation to use your equity unwisely. And don't feel guilty about leaving your equity idle. Idle equity is the best kind.

4. The decision works against your goal of getting out of debt. If you are thinking about getting a shiny new car, a boat, or an RV, or if you're thinking of using a line of equity credit to take an expensive Caribbean vacation, think about what it will do to your budget. You will take on a long series of repayments, and that means staying in debt longer. Is the purchase worth delaying your goal of becoming debt-free?

If you are now committed to a long-term debt, you may

say, "I can't really get out of debt until this is repaid." But you are not limited to repaying any debt on a prescribed schedule. You may be able to accelerate the schedule, reducing interest expense. This action not only achieves your goal, it also helps you to avoid going into debt again. The next chapter gives some final guidelines for taking charge of debt and escaping it permanently.

CHAPTER 11

SETTING YOUR OWN RULES

We are all refugees of a
future that never happened.
—*Lee Weiner*

Your financial future depends on the actions you take today—
to erase your debts, to create a savings plan, and to build assets
instead of spending them. You have the power to set your own
rules.

STAYING OUT OF DEBT

Paying off debts is only the first step. You also need to avoid
repeating past mistakes, to escape the cycle of debt that has
kept you from building a future of your own design. Staying
out of debt demands constant maintenance on several fronts.
You will need to take these actions:

1. Review your goals. Setting financial goals today is a
necessary first step in taking control of your financial situation. However, even the longest-term goal can only be temporary. Your goals will change as you grow, as your income
changes, and as you achieve financial plateaus.

2. Set new goals. One of the pitfalls of goal setting is
that, as you approach the end of the struggle, there is a tendency to lose interest. A goal accomplished or nearly accomplished is far less interesting than the process of getting there.
Avoid this problem by meeting the end of one goal cycle with
new, more up-to-date goals.

3. Recognize the danger signals. Even if you are completely aware of how debt has affected you and your family in the past, you could repeat the mistakes again. You need to watch for the danger signals and be prepared to take immediate action.

4. Anticipate problems in advance. You are in control of your financial health, through your financial plan. An important part of the planning process is to constantly look to the future, not only to achieve positive results, but also to avoid the debt problems that can defeat your goals.

The strategies and plans presented in this book can be used as the building blocks of your personal financial plan. One of the broad assumptions a lot of people make is that financial planning requires professional help. In fact, though, you need to be in charge, to set your own goals, and ensure that they are realized. A financial planner may be helpful when the time comes to invest money, find and buy insurance policies you need, and help you to fill in the gaps in your plan. Those are the best possible ways to use professional help.

THE DANGER SIGNALS

Once you have gained control of your financial situation, be prepared to look for the danger signals in your financial life. These are signs that you may be heading back into trouble:

1. You are no longer exercising control. A little success can spell disaster for your debt management plan. If you find yourself letting your budget controls slip, forgetting to put money into savings, or allowing debts to creep back into your life, it's time to reevaluate and get your controls working again.

2. You borrow money from family and friends. If you find yourself asking for personal loans from family and friends, you could be heading back into debt troubles.

3. You're not keeping your account in balance. In order to stay in charge of your finances, you need to know what's in your bank account; you must keep it balanced every month, without fail.

4. You use the bank float to pay bills. You might depend on the few days checks take to clear the bank. This is called using the float. But it's a dangerous practice that can lead to problems—not only overdrafts, but poor spending habits as well.

5. New bills arrive before old ones are paid. If a new series of bills arrives just as you're finally paying off last month's debts, your budget is slipping from your control. Review the budget and your spending patterns.

6. You aren't opening all of your mail. If you can't bring yourself to open your mail, you also know why. Check your budget, your debt levels, and spending habits. Identify the problem and take steps to reverse it, before it takes you over.

7. Creditors are sending warning notices. You begin receiving second and third notices from creditors because you are not making timely payments or failing to pay past due bills. Do not ignore this significant danger signal.

8. You are delaying sending out checks. You may find yourself doing a juggling act within your checking account. You write checks but delay sending them out because to do so would overdraw your account. It's time to get back to basic planning and budgeting.

9. You are lying to creditors. When you start lying to creditors to delay payment a little longer, that can mean only one thing: You're heading for debt problems and need to reverse the trend.

10. You charge purchases you don't really need. Chronic debt problems often are created not just because of poor budgeting, but because spending itself becomes a habit. Recognize this as a problem, and avoid it in the future.

11. You buy with minimum down payments. When you buy anything on a time plan or arrange financing with the longest possible term, you're heading off course. When you must finance a purchase, set the repayment term based on your budget and not just on what the seller offers you.

12. You are taking cash advances on credit cards. Avoid borrowing money from a credit card company. This is one of the most expensive forms of debt because the interest rate is so high. Rather than using credit cards to live beyond your income, limit your spendings based on your income level.

13. You have reached your credit limit. Set a goal for yourself: You will use charge accounts only to the extent that you will be able to pay the entire balance at the end of the month.

14. Creditors have canceled your accounts. When your accounts are canceled for nonpayment or repeated delays in payment, that's a red flag. It's time to stop charging purchases and prepare a revised budget, to set new goals for yourself, and to bring debts back under control.

15. You have more credit accounts than last year. Getting new credit cards is easy, especially when your payment record is clean. The better you manage your money, the more temptation is placed before you. Don't keep any accounts active except the few that you use regularly.

16. You and your spouse fight about money. There must be countless excuses that people give for fighting about money: "It's not my fault; you're the one who spends the money," or, "You always want things we can't afford," or, "You don't make enough money." But what it all comes down to is that both spouses need to agree to the same program: for spending priorities, for short-term and long-term goals, and for operating from a specific plan.

THE UNLEVERAGED APPROACH

It would be so simple to say, "Never go into debt again." Debt itself is not the problem; it's uncontrolled debt that can and will ruin your financial status. You will no doubt have to finance a new car every few years, the purchase of your home, or your child's college education. If you start your own small business, there may be many occasions where debt is both necessary and smart.

Leading a completely unleveraged life—one in which all of your debts are eliminated permanently—is not practical for very many people. However, some guidelines for going into debt in the future may help you to decide when borrowing is appropriate, and when it is not:

1. Borrow only as part of your plan. "Control" isn't just staying out of debt, or planning so well that you don't ever need to borrow money again. When you enforce the standards you set as part of your personal financial plan, you can plan for future debts when they're appropriate, and avoid any debts that don't fit your plan.

2. Set goals for going into and out of debt. The standards you arrive at and enforce will ultimately determine whether or not you will be able to stay out of the debt cycle. Your debt-related goals (such as financing a home) must be planned over many years. But the plan shouldn't stop only at the point when you go into debt. Organize the plan so that you know when and how you will get out of debt. This rule works regardless of why the debt exists, whether it's a 30-year mortgage or a revolving credit card account.

3. Borrow only to acquire assets. Once you have eliminated the debts that caused problems in the first place, you will be able to avoid the same problems in the future by distinguishing between two types of debt. One, the destructive kind, is undertaken in a distinct pattern. You charge your purchases and build up the obligation so that your debt balances keep growing. The other kind of debt increases your net worth permanently. When you buy a home, for example, you gradually repay the mortgage debt while increasing your home equity.

4. Coordinate borrowing and savings goals. You will recognize a clear relationship between your ability to save and your ability to stay out of debt. Your emergency reserve fund will help you to avoid the month-to-month problems of dealing with unexpected and variable expenses. And the long-term investment savings plan is a financial habit worth cultivating.

Even when you have long-term debts, you may lead an unleveraged financial life. As long as your debts are offset by other assets, you are using debt wisely to build and preserve net worth, rather than spending your income on payments for past purchases.

ELEMENTS OF THE DEBT PLAN

We have proposed the family budget, emergency reserve, and long-term savings, all as part of your plan to get out of debt. You can also plan the use of credit so that your financial plan involves a debt side.

Example: You have three store charge accounts and two credit card accounts. The total credit limit on these accounts is more than $3,000. However, your debt plan includes an important standard: You will never charge more than you can afford to pay when the bill arrives.

Example: You want to buy a home, but you will be making payments on a 30-year mortgage. You compare the cost of renting to the mortgage payment level, adjusted for the tax benefits of deducting interest. Although you will be paying more each month, you will be investing in home equity over a period of many years. Your debt standard: As long as home equity is growing beyond the rate of additional expense, the debt is being properly managed. (And, if the financing is on a fixed-rate basis, inflation works to your benefit as well.)

Example: You decide to accelerate the payments on your mortgage, paying $50 per month more than the required amount. This action will save thousands of dollars in interest and also reduce the repayment term by several years. Your debt standard: As long as you have an adequate emergency reserve fund, acceleration is an excellent way to build equity and reduce interest at the same time. This goal should be coordinated with a desired full repayment date.

Example: You had to pay $1,100 for repairs to your car last month, and you used your credit card to do it. You can't afford to repay the entire amount all at once. Although the minimum payment is only $33, you check your budget and decide to pay $300 per month. In addition, you will not use that credit card until the debt has been paid off. Your debt standard: This is a necessary form of temporary debt. However, repaying the obligation will become a high priority, and additional debts will be avoided at least until this one is paid.

All of these cases show how the budgeting standards you set and follow help to control debt. There will be many times when going into debt—temporarily—cannot be avoided. The problem, though, is not in borrowing money, but in not following a logical plan for repayment . . . or, even worse, in not having a plan at all.

REWARDING YOURSELF

As long as you're entangled in debt and don't take steps to fix the problem, you will continue to punish yourself—by allowing debt to control you, instead of the other way around. Debt can add pressure to your relationships, prevent you from acquiring the luxuries you want and deserve, and ruin your self-esteem. But an equally destructive problem comes up when you don't reward yourself.

As you begin bringing debts under control, you will relieve the financial burdens of the past. But if your rules are so strict that you never have any room in the budget for an occasional treat, then the quality of your life will suffer. As long as you're making progress, why not reward yourself?

Leave some flexibility in your budget to spend money on nonnecessities now and then—even if you must delay the master plan a little longer. There is little enjoyment in eliminating debts if you can't also celebrate your success.

Money should not be the end result or the goal itself. Acquiring money is not really your purpose in financial planning. The proper planning and control of money does give you an important form of freedom, one that many families never really achieve—the freedom to *not* have to worry about financial problems.

To a large extent, the degree to which you can exercise financial freedom defines the quality of your life. If you can't buy the things you need because you've used up credit buying the things you wanted, then you must give up financial freedom. If you cannot pay the fees required for your child's college education because you didn't plan ahead and cannot borrow any more money now, you were not aware of the lesson: Financial freedom isn't automatic; you can reach your goals only through planning.

Misfortunes arise because families do not take steps to get out of debt. Instead, they continue letting the lenders control their lives by granting them easy credit and by allowing the debt level to escalate as income grows, perhaps outpacing it in time. There is nothing mysterious about controlling money, although many people buy into that myth. You don't need any knowledge that you don't already have or superhuman discipline to take control. What you do need is a clear plan with precise goals and the desire to reach those goals.

The process of gaining control over debts may be long and difficult, but the reward is worth the effort. When you do finally reach the point where you are no longer under pressure from creditors, when you avoid borrowing even when it's readily available, and when you achieve even the most difficult financial goals you set, you discover something: You *are* in control, and you do have the power to achieve the financial freedom that everyone wants and deserves.

INDEX